Y0-ABW-455

DIAGNOSING ORGANIZATIONS

Methods, Models, and Processes

Applied Social Research Methods Series
Volume 8

Applied Social Research Methods Series

Series Editor:
LEONARD BICKMAN, Peabody College, Vanderbilt University
Series Associate Editor:
DEBRA ROG, National Institute of Mental Health

This series is designed to provide students and practicing professionals in the social sciences with relatively inexpensive softcover textbooks describing the major methods used in applied social research. Each text introduces the reader to the state of the art of that particular method and follows step-by-step procedures in its explanation. Each author describes the theory underlying the method to help the student understand the reasons for undertaking certain tasks. Current research is used to support the author's approach. Examples of utilization in a variety of applied fields, as well as sample exercises, are included in the books to aid in classroom use.

Volumes in this series:

DIAGNOSING ORGANIZATIONS

Methods, Models, and Processes

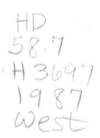

HD
58.7
H3697
1987
West

Michael I. Harrison

**Applied Social Research Methods Series
Volume 8**

SAGE PUBLICATIONS
The Publishers of Professional Social Science
Newbury Park   London   New Delhi

Copyright © 1987 by Sage Publications, Inc.

All rights reserved. No part of this book may be reproduced or utilized in any form or by any means, electronic or mechanical, including photocopying, recording, or by any information storage and retrieval system, without permission in writing from the publisher.

For information address:

SAGE Publications, Inc.
2111 West Hillcrest Drive
Newbury Park, California 91320

SAGE Publications Ltd.
28 Banner Street
London EC1Y 8QE
England

SAGE Publications India Pvt. Ltd.
M-32 Market
Greater Kailash I
New Delhi 110 048 India

Printed in the United States of America

Library of Congress Cataloging-in-Publication Data

Main entry under title:

Harrison, Michael I.
    Diagnosing organizations.

    (Applied social research methods series ; v. 8)
    Bibliography: p.
    Includes index.
    1. Organizational behavior. 2. Organizational change.
I. Title. II. Series.
HD58.7.H3697 1986   302.3′5   86-13078
ISBN 0-8039-2626-X
ISBN 0-8039-2627-8 (pbk.)

FIFTH PRINTING, 1989

CONTENTS

PREFACE

This book introduces the methods, models, and processes of organizational diagnosis. It is intended for advanced undergraduates, graduate students, and other readers having a basic knowledge of behavioral science methods and concepts but limited exposure to the fields of organizational behavior and organization development. Organizational diagnosis involves the use of behavioral science knowledge to assess an organization's current state and to help discover routes to its improvement. Professional consultants (and occasionally participants in an organizational self-study) conduct diagnoses to develop recommendations for handling a particular challenge or problem (e.g., rapid employee turnover) or to contribute to organization development programs aimed more broadly at improving processes (e.g., decision making) and structures (e.g., division of responsibilities) and enhancing organizational effectiveness.

Although this book is mainly directed at would-be practitioners of diagnosis, it develops several themes of concern to professional consultants and applied researchers:

(1) Practitioners need to be as attentive to the relationships that develop between them and the members of the organization being studied as they are to their methods and diagnostic interpretations.
(2) Diagnosis can benefit from using an open-systems approach stressing external relations and resource dependencies, the interdependencies of system parts, and the impacts of structural and organization-level factors. This approach recognizes that many internal and external contingencies determine what managerial practices work best.
(3) Practitioners must acknowledge the political nature of organizations and come to terms with the implications of influence struggles and power relations for consulting practice.

My students at Bar Ilan University and Boston College contributed significantly to this project through their course participation and their reports on organizations in which they worked and conducted research. Yaacov Ben Dor, the head of the consulting firm, TIL, and Nisan Hadas of the Israeli Air Force provided opportunities to engage in diagnostic work, to help others build their diagnostic skills, and to develop my own approach to diagnosis and consulting. Yizhak Samuel of Rafael, Bruce Phillips of General Motors, and my

wife, Jo Ann, of Bar Ilan's School of Education, generously shared
their consulting experiences with me. The groundwork for this book
was laid during a sabbatical spent at the Harvard Business School
and Boston College's School of Management. My thanks to the
academic and administrative staffs of these institutions and of Bar
Ilan for providing me with congenial and stimulating work environments. In particular, thanks to Arthur Turner, who sponsored my
visit to Harvard, provided valuable feedback on my work, and
contributed greatly to my understanding of the impact of interpersonal processes on consulting. Thomas Backer, Jean Bartunek,
Leonard Bickman, Jo Ann Harrison, Dafna Izraeli, Debra Rog, and
one anonymous reader read the entire manuscript and made invaluable suggestions for its improvement. I also benefited from my all-
too-brief association with the late Ed Huse. Judy Gordon, Jim
Bowditch, Dal Fisher, Jack Lewis, Bill Torbert, and my other colleagues
at Boston College and at Bar Ilan also gave valuable advice and
encouragement. Hadassah Rahab, Kumiko DiSalvo, and Clare White-
Sullivan provided invaluable secretarial assistance. Yoshio Saito and
members of the Audio-Visual Department at Boston College kindly
prepared the figures in Chapters 2, 3, and 4.

Finally, I want to express my appreciation to my wife, Jo Ann, who
is a never-failing source of support and inspiration. She and my son,
Natan, helped me keep this project in perspective. This book is
dedicated to them, to my father, my brother, and to the memory of my
mother Joan Kant Harrison.

1

Diagnosis: Approaches and Methods

This chapter examines the main features of diagnosis and its uses in organization development and other forms of behavioral science consulting. Three critical facets of diagnosis are introduced; (1) *The Consulting Process*—working with members of an organization in planning and administering a diagnostic study and providing feedback on the findings; (2) *Interpretation*—defining the problems presented by members of the organization, framing issues for study, and interpreting the findings; and (3) *Methods*—collecting and summarizing diagnostic data.

INTRODUCTION

Organizational diagnosis is the process of using concepts and methods from the behavioral sciences to assess an organization's current state and find ways to increase its effectiveness.[1] Diagnosis can take many forms:

Case 1: Members of a private behavioral-science consulting firm study the overall structure of a large transport company in response to a request from its senior management. The managers were overburdened with minor problems originating in the firm's branches and sought advice on reducing the decision-making burden on top management and improving the coordination of field operations.

Case 2: The head of a national charitable agency asks a member of the agency's Human Resources Department to help top executives learn to work together more effectively. The human resources specialist interviews members of the executive committee in preparation for off-site workshops designed to improve teamwork within the executive committee.

1. The term "behavioral science" refers to both the social and behavioral sciences. Unless otherwise noted the cases in the text are based on actual cases drawn from my own experiences, those of my colleagues, and from the business press and other published sources.

Case 3: A professor of psychology conducts a survey of workers in a manufacturing plant as part of a program cosponsored by union and management to make work more satisfying and rewarding.

All of these cases involved requests by some client for advice from a consultant. *Clients*—like the senior management group in the first case and the union and management representatives in the third— are the people who sponsor a consultation and bear most of the responsibility for implementing its recommendations. The clients thus play a critical role in defining the goals of the consultations and shaping relationships between the consultant and the organization. In these three cases, the clients turned to consultants trained in the behavioral sciences because the clients assumed that the problems or challenges facing their organization related to people, groups, and organizational arrangements rather than involving mainly business or technical issues. Clients often refer initially to problems like these:

—Employee turnover, stress and health problems, low morale, poor work quality, neglect of equipment, and low productivity
—Conflicts and tensions that are polarizing people and groups, mis-understandings, and communication failures
—Disruptions of work flows between groups, tasks falling between the cracks, frequent delays and crises, red tape, and wasteful overlapping of responsibilities
—Missed opportunities (e.g., failure of a marketing campaign), lack of innovation and new ideas, dissatisfaction with the organization among powerful external groups (e.g., major clients) or supervisory bodies (e.g., boards of directors), inability to adjust to changing external conditions (e.g., technologies, markets)

In other cases clients may request an assessment of how well the organization is functioning in some area—such as meeting the career needs of its skilled employees—or they may seek advice on how to improve performance in areas such as technological innovativeness, creativity, productivity, quality, or flexibility in the face of techno-logical change. Concerns and problems like these have led to consul-tations and change projects in public sector organizations such as schools, hospitals, city governments, and the military; private firms in areas such as manufacturing, banking, and retailing; voluntary groups such as charities and religious groups; and cooperative businesses and communities.

The behavioral science *consultants* to whom clients turn are specialists in organization development, applied research, human resources, or related fields who provide advice and other services to members of the organization when requested to do so (see Steele, 1975; Tilles, 1961; Turner, 1982, on the consulting process). Besides being skilled at understanding and investigating organizational life, these consultants are usually skilled at giving feedback and working with groups. The consultants can be located within advisory units of a large organization (e.g., the Human Resources Department in case 2 above) or may be hired from outside on a contractual basis (e.g., cases 1 and 3). External consultants are usually members of management consulting firms or are university faculty members specializing in organizational research and consulting.

In each of the cases described above the consultants (or *practitioners*) conducted a diagnosis to understand the nature and causes of the problems or challenges initially presented by clients, to identify additional organizational problems and opportunities, to discover ways to solve these problems, and to improve *organizational effectiveness*. During diagnosis they compared the *current state* within the client organization to some *preferred state* (e.g., improved coordination of field operations, improved teamwork) and assessed effectiveness in terms of some standard (e.g., employee satisfaction). Moreover, each diagnostic study involved a search for ways to narrow the gap between the current and the desired state of affairs.

In light of the diagnostic findings consultants may recommend changing one or more of the key features of the organization. These include managerial goals or strategies (e.g., to develop a new product); members' skills, knowledge, and attitudes (e.g., interpersonal skills needed for teamwork); interpersonal and intergroup processes (e.g., leadership patterns); organizational structures (e.g., division into departments); and work technologies. Moreover, they may recommend a wide range of *interventions* to accomplish these changes— including training programs and workshops, conflict mediation, redefinition of job responsibilities, changes in pay and other reward systems, and the redesign of work techniques (see "Organization Development Interventions" below).

PLAN OF THE BOOK

This first chapter describes diagnosis and explains its contribution to behavioral science consulting. Then it shows how effective diagnosis depends on managing the *processes and relationships* that develop as consultants work with members of an organization, making appropriate *interpretations* of organizational problems and diagnostic findings and choosing appropriate *methods* for gathering and summarizing diagnostic data. Chapter 2 presents a model of organizations as open systems and shows how the model can help practitioners choose topics for diagnosis, develop criteria for assessing organizational effectiveness, and decide what steps, if any, will help clients solve problems and enhance organizational effectiveness.

Chapters 3 through 5 explain how to diagnose *individual* attitudes and behavior (e.g., work effort), *group-level* factors (e.g., decision making, interpersonal relations), and broader *organizational* patterns. Exercises for students are provided at the end of Chapters 1 through 5. Chapter 6 discusses diagnostic goals and conditions for their attainment and examines ethical and professional issues that confront practitioners of diagnosis. The appendices give more details on diagnostic instruments and suggest ways that readers can further develop their diagnostic skills and learn more about organizational consulting. A more detailed overview of the book can be obtained by reading the overviews at the start of each chapter and the section, "Diagnostic Goals," in Chapter 6.

THE USES OF DIAGNOSIS

Diagnosis and Organization Development

Diagnosis is a crucial part of *organization development*—a term that includes programs of *action research* and *planned change* (Huse & Cummings, 1985). These terms refer to efforts by consultants to use behavioral science knowledge to help clients improve organizational effectiveness. Organization development consultants work with clients and other members of an organization to plan a diagnostic study, gather and analyze data, provide feedback on the findings, and plan actions in response to this feedback (Nadler, 1977). The diagnoses in the cases cited at the beginning of the chapter were all parts of organization development activities. As these cases suggest, organization development consultants usually seek to enhance basic organizational features, such as communication and employee motivation, rather than just trying to solve short-term problems. Thus they seek to build the organization's capacities to handle *future* problems and challenges (see Chapter 6, "Diagnostic Goals").

Stages in organization development. Although organization development activities overlap and interact in practice, it is helpful to distinguish seven main stages that occur in full organizational development projects (Kolb & Frohman, 1970):

Scouting—The consultant(s) and client(s) get to know each other without contracting to carry out a project. The consultant seeks to determine how ready and able the client and other members of the organization are to follow through on a project and to change their behavior and their organization, if necessary. In addition, the consultant forms a first impression of the organization's needs, problems, and capacities and decides whether they fit his or her resources (e.g., time and staff), abilities, and interests.

Entry—The consultant and the client negotiate about their expectations for the project and formalize them in a contract specifying the timing and nature of the consultant's activities; staff and facilities (e.g., computer time) to be supplied by both parties; forms of collaboration; and the expected benefits to all participants in the project.

Diagnosis—The consultant gathers information about the nature and sources of organizational problems and challenges, analyzes this information, examines possible solutions, considers ways to improve effectiveness, and provides feedback to clients (and sometimes to other members of the organization); diagnosis may precede or be intertwined with the next two steps.

Planning—Consultants and clients jointly establish objectives for the project's action phase and plan any steps (interventions) to be taken to solve problems and improve effectiveness.

Action—Clients implement these plans with the help of the consultant.

Evaluation—Clients and consultants assess the impacts of the action phase and consider further actions. Under ideal circumstances an independent researcher evaluates project outcomes.

Termination—The project terminates if no further action is planned. The project may break off earlier if clients or consultants become dissatisfied with it.

Organization development interventions. In light of the diagnostic findings, clients and consultants choose among a wide range of possible interventions during the planning stage of organizational development (see Beer, 1980; Bennis et al., 1976; Burke, 1982; Huse & Cummings, 1985; Tichy, 1983 for surveys). These interventions may aim at one or more of the following types of targets:

Members—changing or selecting for skills, attitudes, and values through training programs and courses (e.g., the management development program in the Southwestern Hospitals case below); recruitment, selection, counseling, and placement, stress management and health-maintenance programs.

Behavior and processes—changing interaction processes, such as decision making, leadership, and communication through sensitivity training, team building (e.g., case 2), process consultation (see below), third-party intervention for conflict resolution; feedback of survey data for self-diagnosis and action planning.

Organizational structures and technologies—redesigning jobs (e.g., case 3), administrative procedures, reward mechanisms, the division of labor, coordinating mechanisms (see Chapter 4), introducing new work procedures (e.g., work teams instead of assembly line in automobile plant).

Organizational goals, strategies, and cultures—promoting goal clarification and the formulation of strategies for coping with markets and other external conditions through workshops and exercises (e.g., "Open Systems Planning" in Chapter 5); changing corporate culture (values, norms, beliefs) to fit strategies and environmental conditions.

A case study. The following case describes the diagnostic stage of an organization-development project and the recommendations made during the planning stage. It illustrates the methods used, the ways in which consultants may redefine the problems presented to them, and the way that diagnosis can lead to recommendations for action.

Southwestern Hospital System (SHS), a nonprofit chain of 12 hospitals, was in serious financial trouble when its top management turned for help to a team of university-based organizational consultants (Tichy, 1978, 1983). SHS asked the consultants for help after their chronic financial problems had become acute as a result of changes in a local employer's health program that had supplied nearly 30% of SHS's revenues. The consultants suggested that they conduct a broad diagnostic study, instead of concentrating on the immediate crisis. Once agreement was reached on the scope and character of the study, the consultants framed their diagnostic study to include underlying managerial and organizational problems that might threaten SHS's long-term viability. Guided by a broad analytical framework (similar to the one described in Chapter 2), they gathered data on SHS's financial and organizational environment and on its major organizational components, including

—management's view of SHS's mission, objectives, and long-term strategy

—SHS's management style (participativeness, flexibility, openness of communication)

—managerial structures and processes (such as conflict resolution procedures, decision making, communication patterns, mechanisms for coordinating work)

—SHS's performance and outputs

The consultants interviewed the hospital heads, directors of nursing, chiefs of the medical staffs, and 14 members of the staff at SHS headquarters. They also studied organizational documents, observed administrative meetings and managerial work, and conducted a questionnaire study among employees. The questionnaire dealt with satisfaction with work, the goals of SHS, conflict resolution techniques, and informal (unofficial) work relations.

After analyzing these data. the consultants concluded that the administrators at SHS needed to become more skilled at analyzing external developments and planning to deal with them. They also found that SHS needed a more flexible organizational structure so that it could better handle the many uncertainties in its environment (see Chapter 4). Hence they recommended that SHS introduce new forms of coordination between the hospitals and the headquarters, create a program of strategic planning, and start a management development program to train administrators to handle their tasks more professionally.

Diagnostic activities outside of the diagnostic stage. Many organization development projects shift back and forth between stages rather than proceeding sequentially. In addition, consultants often engage in diagnostic activities during other stages in a consultation. In the *scouting stage,* for example, to get a feel for interpersonal processes, consultants may closely, but informally, observe interactions between clients and other members of the organization that occur in the consultants' presence. Similarly, they may tour the organization's physical plant and note any unobtrusive indications of working conditions, morale, and performance. On a walk through a corporate headquarters, for instance, an experienced consultant might notice that office workers have not personalized their workspaces with pictures of their families and desk ornaments, as so often occurs. The consultant would then make a mental note to check whether this tendency reflects low identification with the workplace among office workers or a corporate policy forbidding personalization of work stations. During scouting consultants may also conduct a few interviews or discussions with important members in order to become familiar with the organization and to assess the members' attitudes toward the proposed consulting project. They will also read any available documents on the organization's history, purposes, and current operations.

Based on this information consultants usually make a *preliminary diagnosis* of the organization's needs and strengths and its capacity for improvement and change. This preliminary diagnosis is critical to the further development of the project. The experienced practitioner will seek to determine as early as possible whether members of an organization are likely to cooperate with a more formal diagnostic study and how willing and able they are to reach decisions and act in response to feedback. By discussing these first impressions with clients, practitioners can adjust their expectations and those of their clients and avoid entering into a relationship that will become an exercise in frustration for both parties.

In a sense, diagnosis also forms a part of the *action stage* of organization development because it is an *intervention* into the routine life of an organization (Argyris, 1970). The process of asking people about their work and their organization encourages them to examine their own feelings, to think about the way their organization is run, and may lead them to expect that management will act to change things. In *process consultation* (Schein, 1969), for example, the practitioner provides feedback on group processes to heighten awareness of these processes and help improve them. Similarly in Open Systems Planning (see Chapter 5), the consultant helps managers diagnose their organization's environmental position in order to aid decision making and strategy formulation. Many of the issues that arise during diagnosis also become important when consultants and clients move into the *evaluation stage* and try to determine what effects some intervention has had. In light of this evaluation, clients and consultants may negotiate entry into another cycle of diagnosis, planning, and action.

Participation in Diagnosis by Members of the Organization

Advantages and disadvantages. Many organization development projects and other consultations can be described as *consultant-centered* because the consultant takes on most of the responsibility for guiding the project from diagnosis through the planning of proposed actions and may even conduct any interventions or supervise their implementation. Because diagnosis requires technical skills, it often becomes very consultant centered. Once the proposed study is approved, clients and other members of the organization may not be actively involved until they receive feedback on the findings. Practitioners often prefer this type of diagnosis because it seems simpler and more suitable to objective, rigorous research. However, they often discover after giving feedback that their clients regard the study's findings as irrelevant or overly threatening and are unwilling to act upon them (Block, 1981; Turner, 1982; see also Chapter 6).

In contrast, *client-centered* diagnoses involve clients or members appointed by them in as many phases of the study as is feasible (Lawler & Drexler, 1980; Turner, 1982). One benefit of this approach is that members can more readily contribute their insights and expertise about organizational life as they participate actively in gathering and analyzing diagnostic data. In addition, participation often increases members' commitment to the importance of the study and makes the feedback more believable and salient for them. Participation also enhances the possibility that members will develop the capacity to assess their own operations. This capacity for routine self-assessment can help organizations cope with the rapid pace of social, technological, and economic change (Nadler et al., 1976; Torbert, 1981; Wildavsky, 1972). On the other hand, the active involvement of members in diagnosis may raise questions about the study's objectivity and may lead people to fear that their responses or observed behavior will not be kept confidential.

Self-Diagnosis. Members of an organization may be able to conduct a self-diagnosis without the aid of a professional consultant, if they are open to self-analysis and criticism, and if some members have the skills needed for the gathering and interpretation of information. Here is an example of a modest self-diagnosis (Austin et al., 1982, p. 20):

> The executive director of a multi-service youth agency appointed a program-review committee to make a general evaluation of the services provided by the agency and make recommendations for improving its effectiveness. The committee included clinical case workers, supervisors, administrators, and several members of the agency's governing board. The director of the agency, who had technical knowledge of how to conduct such a study, served as an advisor to the committee. She asked the committee members to look first at the agency's intake service, because it was central to the operations of the entire agency

and suffered from high turnover among its paid staff. Besides examining intake operations, the committee members decided to investigate whether clients were getting appropriate services. They interviewed both the paid and the volunteer intake staff and surveyed clients over a three-month period. Their main finding was that there were substantial delays in client referral to counseling. They traced these delays to the difficulties that the half-time coordinator of intake had in handling the large staff, many of whom were volunteers, and to the heavy burden of record keeping that fell on the intake workers. This paperwork was required by funding agencies but did not contribute directly to providing services to clients. In order to increase the satisfaction of the intake staff and thereby reduce turnover, the committee recommended that the coordinator's position be made full time and that the paperwork intake be reduced. The executive director accepted the first recommendation and asked for further study of how to streamline the record-keeping process and reduce paperwork.

As this example suggests, during self-diagnosis members of the organization temporarily take on some of the tasks that would otherwise have been the responsibility of a professional consultant. Many of the interpretive models and research techniques described in this book and in other guides to diagnosis (e.g., Lauffer et al., 1977, 1982; Weisbord, 1978) could be used in such self-studies. People who want to conduct a self-diagnosis or act as consultants should be skilled at handling the interpersonal relationships that develop during a study and at giving feedback to groups and individuals, as well as at gathering and interpreting diagnostic data.

Comparisons to Other Types of Organizational Research

Another way of understanding diagnosis is to contrast it to other forms of investigation into organizational life. As defined here, diagnosis does not include investigations of programs by governmental bodies, comptrollers, ombudsman, journalists, and bodies granting professional certification (e.g., of schools). These studies are not ordinarily grounded in the methods and models of behavioral science and differ from diagnosis in their sponsorship, goals, assumptions, and in the relationships between investigators and members of the focal organization.

Diagnosis has more in common with *evaluation research* (Rossi & Freeman, 1982), in which behavioral science research contributes to the planning, monitoring, and assessment of the costs and impacts of social programs in areas such as health, education, and welfare. Like diagnosis, evaluation is practically oriented, and it may focus on effectiveness. But diagnosis

- —uses many definitions of effectiveness, rather than concentrating on project impacts on some target population (e.g., impact of reading readiness program on preschoolers)
- —focuses more on the organizations delivering goods and services than on their impacts on clients and customers
- —examines operations, processes, and structures more fully, rather than concentrating on whether projects were conducted according to plans

The term *organizational assessment* is sometimes used to describe the gathering of useful data about organizations through social science research techniques (Lawler et al., 1980). Diagnosis is one use of assessment data, but assessment can also refer to other uses, such as helping public and private agencies formulate policies and allocate funds (e.g., to help reduce stress at work) or conducting academic research on organizational variables (e.g., determining the causes of job satisfaction).

Diagnosis differs substantially from *nonapplied, academic research* on organizations in its emphasis on obtaining results that will be immediately useful to members of a client organization (Block, 1981, p. 142). Unlike academic research, diagnostic studies

- —concentrate on the causes of a problem or condition that can be changed most readily, even if these are not the most important or interesting from a researcher's point of view
- —may encourage the members of the organization under study to become involved in the research
- —may have to use impressionistic, unsystematic research methods to conform to practical constraints and client preferences
- —need to rely on hunches, experience, and intuition, as well as scientific methods when analyzing data and formulating conclusions and recommendations
- —cannot remain neutral about the impact of their study on the organization and needs and concerns of members of the organization

These and other differences between diagnosis and nonapplied research can create serious dilemmas for diagnostic practitioners who seek to maintain academic research standards (see Chapter 6).

THREE FACETS OF DIAGNOSIS

To conduct a diagnosis, consultants have to deal simultaneously with issues of *process*, *interpretation*, and *method* and try to achieve an appropriate match between them. Thus, for example, consultants may choose a data-gathering technique, such as observing work on a shop floor, because that method is less likely than others (e.g., questionnaires) to encourage speculations that changes will soon occur in the plant. The discussion that follows highlights important features of the three facets of diagnosis and the relations among them.

Process

Phases in diagnosis. In some diagnoses consultants simply provide feedback on the state of the organization and leave decisions about appropriate actions up to clients, whereas in others they recommend one or more specific interventions. In either case the diagnostic tasks, techniques, and the relationships between clients and the organization shift as the diagnosis moves through a series of phases that are roughly analogous to the stages of organization development discussed above (see also Nadler, 1977):

> *Scouting*—Clients and consultants explore expectations for the study, client presents problems, challenges; consultant assesses likelihood of cooperation with various types of research, probable receptiveness to feedback, makes a preliminary reconnaissance of organizational problems and strengths.
> *Contracting*—Consultants and clients negotiate and agree on the nature of the diagnosis and the consulting relationship.
> *Study design*—Methods, measurement procedures, sampling, analysis, and administrative procedures are planned.
> *Data gathering*—Data are gathered through interviews, observations, questionnaires, analysis of secondary data, group discussions and workshops.
> *Analysis*—The data are organized and summarized; consultants (and sometimes clients) interpret them and prepare for feedback.
> *Feedback*—The consultants present their findings to clients and other members of the client organization. Feedback may include explicit recommendations or more general findings to stimulate discussion, decision making, and action planning.

As the following case suggests, these phases may not occur sequentially in practice and may overlap:

The owner and president of 21C Scientific Instruments, a small manufacturing firm, asked a private consultant to examine ways to improve efficiency and morale. They agreed that a set of in-depth interviews would be conducted with divisional managers and a sample of other employees. The first interviews with top managers suggested that their frustrations and poor morale stemmed from the firm's lack of growth and the president's failure to include the managers in decision making and strategy formulation. In light of these findings the consultant returned to the president, discussed the results of these interviews and suggested refocusing the diagnosis on the relationships between the managers and the president and on planning and strategy formulation within the firm.

In this case analysis and feedback began before the data gathering phase was completed. In addition the diagnosis shifted back into the contracting phase when the consultant sought approval to redefine the diagnostic problem and change the research design.

Key process issues. The relationships that develop between practitioners and members of a client organization can greatly affect the outcomes of an organizational diagnosis, just as they affect other aspects of consulting (Block, 1981; Turner, 1982). Although clients and practitioners should try to define their expectations early in the project, they will often have to redefine their relationship during the course of the diagnosis so as to deal with issues that were neglected during initial contracting or arose subsequently.[2] To manage the consulting relationship successfully, practitioners need to handle the following key process issues (see Nadler, 1977; Van de Ven & Ferry, 1980, pp. 22–51) in ways that promote cooperation between themselves and members of the client organization:

Purpose—What are the goals of the study, how are they defined, and how can the outcomes of the study be evaluated? What issues, challenges, and problems are to be studied?

Design—How will members of the organization be affected by the study design (organizational features to be studied, units and individuals included in the data-gathering, and types of data collection techniques)?

Support and cooperation—Who sponsors and supports the study, and what resources will the client organization contribute? What are the attitudes of other members of the organization toward the study?

2. Suggestions like these that are addressed to consultants (or practitioners) are intended for would-be and beginning practitioners as well as more experienced ones.

Participation—What will be the role of members of the organization in planning the study, gathering the data, interpreting them, and reacting to them?

Feedback—When, how, and in what format will feedback be given? Who will receive feedback on the study and what uses will they make of the data?

The challenge of successfully handling these issues will become apparent as we elaborate on them below and in subsequent chapters.

Interpretation

The second facet of diagnosis involves defining the diagnostic problems, choosing topics for study, and interpreting the results. The importance of *interpretation* was illustrated in the Southern Hospital Systems case, in which the consultants went beyond the initial definition of the organization's problem as an immediate financial crisis and *redefined* that problem as a chronic failure to cope with external conditions. As is often the case, this redefinition contained an image of the organization's desired state, helped specify the issues that should be studied in depth, and even suggested ways that the clients could deal with the problem. In formulating their recommendations the consultants also had to consider which possible solutions were more likely to be accepted and successfully implemented by their clients (see Chapter 2, "Assessing the Feasibility of Change. . .").

Interpretive questions. The following summary of questions that consultants can ask themselves (based partly on Beckhard, 1969, p. 46, and Block, 1981, p. 143) highlights this process of interpretation. The term "problem" is used here to cover any kind of gap between actual and ideal conditions, including challenges to enter new fields, raise standards, and so on.

(1) *Interpreting the initial statement of the problem*—How does the client initially define the problems, needs, and challenges facing the organization or unit? How does the client view the desired state of the organization?

(2) *Redefining the problem*—How can the problem be redefined so that it can be investigated and workable solutions developed? What assumptions about the preferred state of the organization and definitions of organizational effectiveness will be used in the diagnosis? How will solving the problem contribute to organizational effectiveness? What aspects of organizational life will be the focal points of the diagnosis?

(3) *Understanding the current state*—What individuals, groups, and components of the organization are most affected by this redefined problem and most likely to be involved in or affected by its solution? What is their current state? How is the problem currently being dealt with? How do members of the relevant groups define the problem and suggest solving it? What organizational resources and strengths could help contribute to solving the problem and improving effectiveness?

(4) *Identifying the forces for and against change*—What internal and external groups and conditions create pressure for organizational change and what are the sources of resistance to it? How ready and capable of changing are the people and groups who are most affected by the problem and its possible solutions? Do they have common interests or needs that could become a basis for working together to solve the problem?

(5) *Developing workable solutions*—Which behavior patterns and organizational arrangements, if any, can be most easily changed to solve problems and improve effectiveness? What are the best ways to introduce these changes?

In some diagnoses responsibility for the fourth and fifth task is left entirely up to clients and members of the organization (see Chapter 6). Even in such cases, however, the analysis and feedback may reflect practitioners' assumptions about how to improve the organization.

Level of analysis. A major interpretive issue facing consultants concerns the level of analysis at which they will examine a problem and suggest dealing with it. Questions about people's attitudes, motivations, and work behavior focus on the *individual level*. Those dealing with face-to-face relationships are at the *interpersonal level*. At the *group level* are questions about the performance and practices of departments or work units, like those raised in the case of the youth agency self-study. Then come questions at the *divisional level* about the management of major subunits (divisions, branches, factories) within large organizations and about relations between units within divisions. Finally, some investigations, like the study of South-western Hospital Systems, examine the *organization* as a whole and its relation to its environment.

Many important phenomena show up at more than one level of analysis. In a manufacturing division, for example, the main technology (work methods and techniques) might be an assembly line. At the group level, each work group would have its own assembly techniques and equipment. At the individual level there are specific assembly procedures and the equipment used by each particular employee.

Certain other phenomena, like the aggressiveness of a firm's pursuit of new markets, can best be observed at a particular level—in this case the organizational level of analysis.

The choice of levels of analysis in diagnosis should reflect the nature of the problem, the goals of the diagnosis, and the organizational location of the clients. To facilitate the diagnosis and increase the chances that recommendations will be implemented, practitioners should concentrate on organizational features over which their clients have considerable control. Changes in the departmental structure of an entire division, for example, could be made only with the support of top management. In addition consultants should focus their diagnosis on levels at which interventions are most likely to lead to organizational improvement. For example, if managers asked for a diagnosis of problems related to employee performance, consultants would examine the rules and procedures for monitoring, controlling, and rewarding performance, if these *design tools* (see Chapter 4) could be readily changed by managerial clients. Other influential factors, such as workers' informal relations and their expectations about how hard they should work, might be more difficult to change.

Sometimes by raising or lowering the level of analysis consultants and clients can discover relationships and possibilities for change that were not previously apparent. For instance, rather than concentrating exclusively on leadership, group norms, and relationships within a single, underproductive work group, consultants might look at the work flow of the entire division in which the group was located and examine divisionwide mechanisms for coordinating and controlling performance.

Scope. Practitioners must also decide on the scope of their study. An individual-level diagnosis of broad scope, for example, would try to take into account all of the major factors related to the performance and feelings of the people within a focal unit (see Chapter 3). In contrast, a more narrowly focused individual-level diagnosis within the same unit might look only at those factors that are related to employees' plans to leave their current jobs.

Guides to interpretation. To decide what to study and how to interpret the diagnostic findings, consultants draw on their own professional experience, that of other consultants (as reported in conferences and in print), and on behavioral science methods, findings, and models. Analytical models like the one used in the Southwestern Hospital Systems diagnosis and those presented in the next four chapters can help consultants define and measure organizational effectiveness and identify conditions promoting effectiveness (Tichy, 1983).

Although research-based models can help guide diagnosis, they cannot specify in advance exactly what practitioners should study, how to interpret diagnostic data, or what interventions will work best in a particular client organization. The research behind these models shows that the managerial practices and organization patterns that promote effectiveness for one organization may not do so for another one facing different conditions. The kinds of rules and clear definitions of responsibilities that produce efficiency and high productivity in a state employment agency, for example, probably would not produce these results in a private job placement agency providing custom services to professionals and high-level managers. The chapters that follow point to some of the important *contingencies* that determine what practices work best, but a book of this length cannot adequately discuss all of them (see Fottler, 1981; Kanter & Brinkerhoff, 1981; Khandwalla, 1977; Lorsch & Morse, 1974; Miles & Snow, 1978; Mintzberg, 1979). Among the contingencies that may affect the sources of organizational effectiveness and the appropriateness of particular interventions are the following:

—organizational size and complexity
—overall purpose (e.g., profit versus service)
—sectoral or institutional setting (e.g., social welfare military, manufacturing, banking)
—technological type (individual unit, small batch, mass production; continuous production, e.g., chemicals)
—routineness of procedures
—workforce composition (e.g., occupational, educational, and skill levels)
—degree of bureaucratization
—stage in the organizational life cycle (starting up, established, declining, etc.)
—strategy for coping with the environment
—environmental predictability and competitiveness

In addition, because effectiveness can be defined in many ways (see Chapter 2), there is no single, ideal state for all organizations. Hence, consultants use many divergent models in diagnosis and recommend a wide range of intervention techniques for promoting effectiveness. So far, the virtues of most of these models and interventions have only been demonstrated in a preliminary fashion (see

Alderfer, 1977; Katz & Kahn, 1978; Strauss, 1976). In view of this situation, the chapters that follow seek to convey the range of choices open to practitioners of diagnosis. Models that take account of important contingencies and allow for different definitions of effectiveness (e.g., Lawrence & Lorsch, 1969) are preferred to those advocating some "one best way" to achieve effectiveness (e.g., Blake and Mouton, 1964; Likert, 1967). Special emphasis is given to models for examining organizational and division-level factors, such as organization-environment relations and the fits between organizational structures and technologies (see Chapters 4 and 5). This emphasis reflects the growing recognition in organizational studies (e.g., Miles, 1980) of the powerful impact of such factors on organizational effectiveness.

Methods

Table 1 provides an overview of the data-collection techniques frequently used in diagnosis and provides references for further study. As the table suggests, when choosing techniques for gathering and analyzing data consultants need to consider their implications for the consulting process and their appropriateness to the interpretive questions being asked, as well their practicality and their suitability from a more purely methodological standpoint. Consultants can use some techniques, such as interviewing and the conducting of workshops, to build an understanding of the purposes of the consulting project and sympathy with it. The impact of particular methods on the consulting process will depend, of course, on the ways in which members of the client organization react to them. In some cases, for example, methods like unstructured observations or the conducting of group interviews that do not yield quantified results may be regarded as unscientific. In others, the use of questionnaires or other techniques that lend themselves to quantification may be regarded as too impersonal and overly academic.

Key interpretive issues for consideration include the appropriateness of the method to the topic under study and to the level of analysis. Questionnaire data, for example, lend themselves most readily to examining individual-level attitudes and behavior, whereas observations and interviews can more readily be used to obtain data on interpersonal, group, and organizational factors (see Chapters 3-5).

More strictly methodological considerations concern the degree to which the gathering and analysis procedures are *structured* and *rigorous*. Structured techniques, like fixed-choice questionnaires and observations using a standard coding scheme, follow detailed rules and procedures that facilitate the summarizing of results according to precisely defined categories. Structured data-gathering and measurement procedures usually produce higher levels of reliability (i.e., reproducibility) between investigators, but it is very hard to structure techniques for assessing many complex phenomena, such as the degree to which managers accurately interpret external developments. Rigorous methods (which need not be quantitative) follow accepted standard of scientific inquiry. They have a high probability of producing results that are valid and could be replicated by other trained investigators. Nonrigorous approaches may yield valid results, but these cannot be evaluated or replicated by other investigators. Organization-development consultants may nonetheless use nonrigorous methods because of constraints on resources and access to data or because they feel that the nonrigorous methods contribute to the consulting relationships—for example, by facilitating a more client-centered diagnosis or by enabling them to draw on their professional judgment.

TABLE 1
A Comparison of Methods for Gathering Diagnostic Data*

Method	Advantages	Disadvantages
Questionnaires Self-administered schedules of questions with fixed-choice responses (see Chapter 3; App. B; Bowditch & Buono, 1982; Selltiz et al., 1981).	Easy to quantify and summarize results; quickest and least costly way to gather new data rigorously; suitable for large samples; useful for repeated measures over time, comparisons between units or to norms; standardized instruments contain pretested items and reflect diagnostic models; well-suited for studying attitudes.	Hard to obtain data on structure, behavior, etc., little information on contexts, situations shaping behavior; not suited for subtle or sensitive issues; impersonal; risks of nonresponse, biased answers, invalid questions; requires skills in constructing instruments and quantitative analysis; danger of over-reliance on standard instruments.

Interviews
Interviewer poses open-ended questions according to fixed schedule, interview guide (list of topics) or on-the-spot judgment (see Chapter 2, 3, 5, App. A; Cannell & Kahn, 1968; Schatzman & Strauss, 1973; Selltiz et al., 1981).

Readily cover wide range of topics and features; can be modified to fit needs before or during interview; can convey empathy, build trust; rich data; provide understanding of respondent's own viewpoint and interpretations.

Expensive, require skilled interviewers; sampling problems in large organizations; respondent and interviewer bias; noncomparability of responses in unstructured or semistructured interviews; difficult to analyze and interpret results.

Observations
Observations of people and their work settings (see Chapter 3; Lofland, 1973; Perkins et al., 1981; Schatzman & Strauss, 1973).

Data on behavior are independent of people's generalizations, feelings, opinions; information on effects of situations; flexible, rich data on range of hard-to-measure topics; generate insights and new hypotheses.

Constraints on access are (timing, distance, secrecy, participants' objections); sampling problems; costly, require trained observers; observers bias/reliability; may affect behavior of those observed; problems of interpretation, analysis, reporting; may seem unscientific.

Secondary Analysis
Use of organizational documents, reports, files, unobtrusive measurements (e.g., rate of suggestion box use) (see Chapter 2; Selltiz et al., 1981; Webb et al., 1966).

Unobtrusive, members do not feel or react to measurement; often quantifiable; repeated measures can show change; members of organizations can help gather, analyze data; validity and believability of familiar measures (e.g. wastage); often cheaper and faster than collecting new data; can provide data on total organization and environment.

Access, retrieval, analysis problems can raise costs and time requirements; validity and believability may be low and interpretation difficult when data are not used for original purpose; need to interpret in context; limited coverage of many topics.

| *Workshops and Group Discussions* Discussions on group processes, history, challenges directed or facilitated by consultant or leader; simulations and exercises (see Chapter 5; Schein, 1969). | Useful data on complex, subtle processes; interactions can stimulate thinking; data available for immediate feedback and analysis; high involvement of members of organization; self-diagnosis possible; can feed directly into action planning; consultant can convey empathy, build trust. | Biases due to group processes (e.g., stifling of unpopular views) and leaders' influence; requires group skills; depends on high levels of trust and cooperation within group; impressionistic, not rigorous, may produce superficial, biased results. |

*Derived in part from Bowditch & Buono (1977, pp. 32–33). Nadler (1977, p. 119). Sutherland (1978, p. 163).

No single method for gathering and analyzing data can suit every diagnostic problem and situation, just as there cannot be a universal model for guiding diagnostic interpretations or one ideal procedure for managing the consulting process. By using several methods to gather and analyze their data, practitioners can compensate for many of the drawbacks associated with relying on a single method. They will also need to choose methods that fit the diagnostic problems and contribute to cooperative, productive consulting relationships.

EXERCISE

It will be easier and more satisfying for you to base all of the exercises in this book on the same organization. In addition to organizations where you work or where you know someone who can help you get access to information and people, consider the possibility of studying some part of the university, such as the housing office or the student union, or one of the many voluntary organizations found on campus and in the community. Once you have located an organization or unit (e.g., department, branch), discuss the possibility of studying it with a person who could give you permission to do so and could help you learn about the organization. Explain that you want to do several exercises designed to help you learn how behavioral science consultants and researchers can help organizations deal with issues and challenges confronting them and contribute to their improvement. Promise not to identify the organization and explain that your reports will only be read by your instructor.

If your contact expresses interest in becoming a client—in the sense of wanting to get feedback from your project—explain that you will be glad to provide oral feedback to the contact person only, provided that the anonymity of the people studied can be preserved. During these discussions try to learn as much about your contact person's job, his or her view of organizational affairs, degree of interest in your project, and how much help you can expect from this person. If possible, ask your contact person to take you on a tour of the organization's headquarters or physical plant, and to try to give you an overview of the organization's operations.

Next, imagine that you are going to conduct an organizational diagnosis. What have you learned during your "scouting" that bears on items 1 and 2 in the Interpretive Questions listed in the chapter? Pay particular attention to the way your contact person defined the organization's problems and strengths. Do any alternative interpretations occur to you? Summarize your experiences and understandings so far in a report on the following topics:

(1) Description of the organization and the contact person (including source of access to them)
(2) Initial contacts—including your feelings and behavior and those of the contact person
(3) Your contact peron's view of the organization's strengths, weaknesses, current problems, desired state (see topic 1 of the Interpretive Questions)
(4) Your understanding of these issues (see topic 2 in the Interpretive Questions)
(5) Preliminary thoughts about conducting a diagnosis—topics, methods, groups and individuals to be included

2

Using the Open System Model

A model of organizations as open systems is presented that can help practitioners choose topics for diagnosis, develop criteria for assessing organizational effectiveness, and decide what steps, if any, will help clients solve problems and enhance organizational effectiveness. A list of Basic Organizational Information to gather at the start of a diagnosis is provided, and methods are discussed for gathering and analyzing data in both broad and focused diagnoses.

THE ORGANIZATION AS AN OPEN SYSTEM

The open systems approach provides practitioners with an abstract model that is applicable to any kind of organization and to divisions or departments within them (Beer, 1980; Hall, 1982; Katz and Kahn, 1978; Kotter, 1978; Miles, 1980; Nadler & Tushman, 1980). One useful version of this model is shown in Figure 1.

System Elements

Here are the main elements in the model and their key sub-components:

Inputs (or resources)—This includes the raw materials, money, people ("human resources"), information, and knowledge that an organization obtains from its environment and that contribute to the creation of its outputs.

Outputs—This includes the products, services, and ideas that are the outcomes of organizational action. An organization transfers its main outputs back to the environment and uses others internally.

Technology—This includes the methods and processes for transforming resources into outputs. These methods may be mental (e.g., exercising medical judgment), as well as physical (e.g., drug therapy), and mechanical (e.g., computerized data processing).

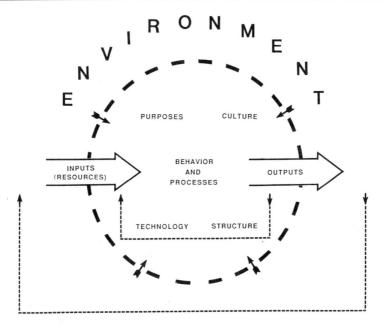

NOTE: Dotted lines show feedback loops.

Figure 1: Organizations as Open Systems

Environment—The *Task Environment* includes all the external organizations and conditions that are directly related to an organization's main
operations and its technologies. They include suppliers, unions, customers, clients, regulators, competitors, markets for products and
resources, and the state of knowledge concerning the organization's
technologies. The *General Environment* includes institutions and conditions that may have infrequent or long-term impacts on the organization and its task environment, including the economy, the legal
system, the state of scientific and technical knowledge, social institutions such as the family, population distribution and composition, the
political system, and the national culture within which the organization operates.

Purposes—This includes the strategies, goals, objectives, plans, and interests
of the organization's dominant decision makers. *Strategies* are overall
routes to goals, including ways of dealing with the environment (e.g.,
strategy for expanding operations into the construction business);
goals are desired end states (e.g., becoming the leading construction
firm in the South), whereas *objectives* are specific targets and indicators
of goal attainment (e.g., 5% growth per year). *Plans* specify courses of

action toward some end. Purposes may be explicit or implicit in the decision makers' actions. They are the outcomes of conflict and negotiation among powerful parties within and outside the organization.

Behavior and processes—This includes the prevailing patterns of behavior, interactions, and relationships between groups and individuals—including cooperation, conflict, coordination, communication, controlling and rewarding behavior, influence and power relations, supervision, leadership, decision making, problem solving, planning, goal setting, information gathering, self-criticism, evaluation, and group learning.

Culture—This includes shared norms, beliefs, values, symbols, and rituals relating to key aspects of organizational life, such as the nature and identity of the organization, the way work is done, the value and possibility of changing or innovating, and relationships between lower and higher ranking members.

Structure—This includes enduring relations between individuals, groups, and larger units—including role assignments (job descriptions; authority, responsibility, privileges attached to positions); grouping of positions in divisions, departments and other units; standard operating procedures; established mechanisms for handling key processes such as coordination (e.g., committees, weekly meetings); human resources mechanisms (career lines, reward, evaluation procedures); actual patterns (e.g., informal relations, cliques, coalitions, power distribution) that may differ from officially mandated ones.

Key Features of the Model

The model contains several important ideas for diagnosis:

(1) *External conditions influence the flow of inputs (resources) to organizations, affect the reception of outputs, and can directly affect internal operations*—for instance, when regulatory agencies define production standards. Figure 1 depicts the possibility for direct impacts on internal operations by showing a broken, permeable boundary around the organization. Feedback from outputs to inputs occurs when responses by customers or clients to products or services affect resource flows—for instance, when demand for cigarettes dropped among American men because they recognized the health hazards of smoking.

(2) *Organizations use many of their products, services, and ideas as inputs to organizational maintenance or growth* (as shown in Figure 1 by the feedback loop within the organizational boundary). A computer firm, for example, may use its own machines and software, and a university may employ its doctoral students as instructors. The

human consequences of work—including members' satisfactions with the quality of their working life and their motivations to contribute to the organization—are another form of output that has important *internal* impacts (see Chapter 3).

(3) *Organizations are influenced by their members as well as their environments.* The employees and clients who enter an organization may contribute to its operations, resist them, or change them from within. In organizations in which the main job involves educating, classifying, or treating people, the same people who enter it are ultimately transferred back to the environment—hopefully healthier, wealthier, or wiser. While these clients are being treated or receiving services, they may change or shape the very practices that were designed to influence them. Current values and standards increasingly urge managers to consider what is good for their employees and clients and not to treat them as inanimate resources (e.g., Business Week, 1981a).

(4) *The eight system elements and their subcomponents are interrelated and influence one another.* An organization's culture and structure affect members' behavior, but their behavior also shapes the structure and the culture. Environments shape purposes, but organizations also shape their environments. Practitioners should therefore be on the watch for nonobvious relations between system features so that they can better anticipate the likely impacts of changes in some part of the organization. They should consider the possibility, for example, that managers may acquire a new computer system to enhance efficiency in record-keeping and accounting, but that once the system is installed, people will start looking for new ways to use it. Thus, technology may shape objectives as well as responding to them.

(5) *Organizations are constantly changing as relationships among their system elements shift.*[1] An organization's responses to internal and external changes depend on members' interpretations of these changes and their decisions about how to deal with them. Information about internal and external developments flows through both official and unofficial channels. Small changes in one part of the system may not require more than routine adjustments in other elements, but major changes in one element can set off a series of changes in others. For instance, if a firm hires people with somewhat less training than past recruits, current procedures for placing and training new employees may still be used with slight adjustments. On the other hand, if the firm sets up a branch overseas and begins to hire people who have radically different backgrounds than those employed at home, major shifts may be needed in the technology, structure, and processes in order to adapt to the employees' skills, experience, and work styles.

1.   The assumption that systems seek a state of "balance" has been widely criticized (e.g., Abrahamsson, 1977) and has been avoided here.

(6) *An organization's success depends heavily on its ability to adapt to its environment—or to find a favorable environment in which to operate—as well as on its ability to tie people into their roles in the organization, conduct its transformative processes, and manage its operations* (Katz & Kahn, 1978). These "system needs" do not necessarily correspond to the interests or priorities of top management (see "How to Choose Effectiveness Criteria," later in this chapter).

(7) *Any level or unit within an organization can be viewed as a system.* So far the model has only been applied to the total organization, but a major division or branch within an organization can also be viewed as a system having all of the elements and features mentioned above. Even a single department or work group within a department can be analyzed as a subsystem embedded within the larger systems. The broader organizational conditions shape the operations of such subunits but do not fully determine them.

Using the System Model

The open system model provides practitioners with a comprehensive yet flexible guide to examining the main features of an organization and understanding their relationships.

Basic organizational information. Drawing on the model (and on Levinson, 1972, pp. 55–59), we generated the following list of basic information about a client organization (or subunit) to gather at the beginning of a diagnosis. After obtaining the overview provided by this information, consultants can decide what topics, if any, they want to study in greater depth. The basic information that is most readily available should be gathered during scouting, and the rest of this information should be collected as quickly as possible after contracting to conduct a diagnosis.

Basic Organizational Information.

(1) *Outputs*—main products or services, volume of sales, production, services delivered etc.; human "outputs" (indications of satisfaction and commitment such as absenteeism, turnover).

(2) *Purposes*—official statements of goals and mission; actual priorities as indicated by budget allocations to divisions, programs (e.g., percentage of budget allocated to research and development).

(3) *Inputs*—financial assets, capital assets including real estate, physical plant, equipment (amount, condition, e.g., age, degree of obsolescence, state of repair); revenues and allocations from funding sources (e.g., for public agencies); human resources—numbers of employees by job category, social and educational backgrounds, training and previous experience.

(4) *Environment*—affiliation and ownership (public, versus private, affiliation with larger bodies and nature of regulation by them); industry; task environment, including major markets, customers, clients; suppliers, competitors, regulators, distributors etc.; availability of funds for growth and expansion (internal and external borrowing, grants and budget prospects for public agencies); physical and social surroundings (e.g., city center versus suburban location, transportation, access to services, neighborhood safety).

(5) *Technology*—type of production (unit, batch, mass, continuous process), level of automation, use of sophisticated information-processing technologies; main procedures used to treat or process people in service organizations; data on operational failures, accidents, waste, down time, etc.

(6) *Structure*—major divisions and units; number of levels of hierarchy; basis for grouping of units (e.g., by functions, markets, see Chapter 4), coordination mechanisms; spans of control (number of subordinates reporting directly to each supervisor); spatial distribution of units, employees, and activities; unions and other forms of employee representation, grievance procedures; human resources policies and procedures (recruitment, selection, orientation, training, placement and promotion, pay, health, safety, benefits); recent union contracts and other obligations affecting human resources management (e.g., directives relating to hiring minorities); informal power blocks and coalitions.

(7) *Behavior and processes*—main processes for high-level decision making, strategy formulation, and planning; major types of conflicts—e.g., labor relations, conflicts between divisions; strength of unions and degree of militancy, union involvement in issues other than compensation; communication styles (e.g., oral, written, meeting oriented).

(8) *Culture*—symbols of organizational identity (logo, slogans, current advertising campaigns, physical appearance of corporate headquarters and branches); myths (stories of founders, historic successes); rituals (outings, sporting events, celebrations, annual reviews and plans); jargon (frequently used terms and phrases); dominant styles of dress, decor, life style; clients' working styles (e.g., taking work home, working overtime).

(9) *System dynamics*—overall financial condition—profits, losses, deficits; growth and contractions (e.g., layoffs, consolidations of units) of inputs, outputs, operating budget; major changes in any of above features.

Using the system model in broad diagnoses. Practitioners who intend to conduct a broad diagnosis can first obtain as much of the Basic Organizational Information as possible and then gather data in greater depth on each of the eight system elements and their relationships. The consultants in the Southern Hospital Systems case (see Chapter 1) used a systems approach like this to decide what topics to study. Then they assessed the degree of fit between system elements like structure and environment (see Chapter 4, "Diagnosing System Fits").

Using the model in focused diagnoses. To apply the model to more narrowly focused diagnoses, practitioners should first gather the Basic Organizational Information so as to better understand the context of the focal problem or issue. Then they can choose the appropriate level(s) of analysis, the system elements most directly related to the focal problem, particular subcomponents within these elements, and the units in which data will be gathered. In data gathering and analysis, practitioners should examine the impacts of *all* eight system elements on the focal problem. Suppose, for example, that the head of a firm that was having trouble retaining top quality engineers in its research and development division asked an internal consultant to study the division's compensation policies. Focusing on the division as a whole, the consultant could examine current compensation policies (a subcomponent of its structure) and the relations between these policies and all eight system elements. Important relations to environmental factors, for instance, would be evident in the ability of the current benefits package to compete with that of other firms recruiting from the same labor pool. Processual impacts would show up in the kinds of behavior and activities that were rewarded (e.g., were promotions going to more innovative engineers or to those who just met deadlines and handled routine problems?).

Redefining presented problems. The systems model can also help practitioners redefine the problems or challenges initially presented by clients. Redefinition occurs whenever consultants assume that presented problems may be symptomatic of broader, underlying conditions and then examine these conditions. In broad studies, like the Southwestern Hospital Systems diagnosis, the decision to examine all system elements and their relations implies an assumption that presented problems, such as falling revenues, reflect complex relations between system elements and will probably require interventions that change these relations. In more focused diagnoses as well, the examination of the links between a presented problem and all system elements can reveal underlying causes or suggest ways to solve the problem that were not considered by the client. The division manager struggling with high turnover among engineers, for example, may not have considered the possibility that a reward system that discouraged innovation and initiative could cause the more creative engineers to look elsewhere for challenging work.

By discovering such unrecognized linkages, consultants can help clients break out of familiar ways of interpreting and responding to problems and may discover solutions that are more feasible than those previously considered (e.g., reward creative work, rather than raising salaries across the board). Although helpful, the open systems model will not suggest exactly how to redefine a problem or how to go about solving it. Insights will typically derive more from past consulting experience and training, from ideas generated by members of the organization, and from the leads provided by some of the more explicit diagnostic models discussed in subsequent chapters.

Data collection. Practitioners can begin gathering the Basic Organizational Information listed above during site visits and initial meetings with clients during scouting (see Chapter 1). Statistics on topics such as budgets, work force composition, financial position, and the scope of operations can be found in organizational documents or can be prepared for the practitioner as soon as the contracting stage has been completed. Official statements of purpose and charts of the organizational structure should also be obtained. Site visits can provide some impressions of the organizational culture, such as the corporate image presented to visitors and employees by buildings, equipment, and furnishings (e.g., "high-tech" versus "tried and true" communications equipment; signs of prosperity and expansion versus signs of retrenchment and cost-cutting). Subsequent investigations will be needed, however, to determine whether these images reflect everyday practice. Bulletin boards and newsletters provide additional unobtrusive indications of organizational culture and processes. For instance, notices about sporting teams whose membership cuts across ranks point to informal contacts between ranks and may indicate a deemphasis of status differences among employees.

High-level managers or their assistants are usually asked to provide basic information. Then further interviews with top managers, department or division heads, and a sample of other members can provide more adequate data on those system features that were not adequately covered initially, such as organizational processes or members' assessments of how well things work in the organization. A schedule like the General Orientation Interview in Appendix A could be used to cover characteristics of units and some broader organizational factors, or a schedule could be created that concentrates on organizationwide features. Interviews with informed outsiders (e.g., journalists or customers) and external documents (newspapers, government reports, etc.) can provide additional data sources on the organization and its external relations.

Measurement problems. Because some of the factors covered in the Basic Organizational Information list and the General Orientation Interview are abstract and hard to measure, practitioners must often content themselves with nonrigorous measures. For instance, when analyzing basic information about the organizational culture of a firm, a practitioner might make a judgment as to the orientation toward employees conveyed in newsletters or other documents (e.g., hard-nosed and competitive versus caring and supportive) without systematically coding the contents of the documents or interviewing managers and employees about human resources policies. Use of more rigorous but time-consuming methods could only be contemplated if the topic were particularly critical to the diagnosis. In like manner, practitioners often have to settle for global assessments of very complex conditions. When interviewing top management, for example, practitioners may ask for general assessments of the organization's overall financial condition (ranging from excellent down to critical), the competitiveness of the environment, and its degree of threat or munificence.

Consultants can learn a great deal about their respondents' viewpoints and can identify controversial or problematic issues for further study by comparing their respondents' interpretations of such complex organizational and environmental conditions. They can also gain insights of this sort by comparing respondents' descriptions of ostensibly objective phenomena, such as the lines of authority and reporting. If, for example, departmental managers draw different organization charts of the same division, this diversity points to ambiguity and possibly to conflict about the lines of authority and the division of labor in that division. By using two or more types of data on the same topic (e.g., descriptions of corporate goals in the report to stockholders and in interviews) practitioners can also illuminate the perspectives and concerns of individuals and groups and can develop their own independent judgments about topics on which participants hold divergent views.

Summarizing and analyzing data. The lists of Basic Organizational Information and of System Elements can serve as accounting schemes

within which consultants can organize and summarize their diagnostic findings. One straightforward approach is to make a separate
card or file for each system element and then to enter information
into appropriate files, cross-referencing them as needed, and noting
the source of the information. A typical entry in the Technology file
for a diagnostic study of a high school might read as follows:

> Teaching techniques—most classes are lectures and discussions con-
> ducted by teacher, supplemented by homework exercises and projects.
> Remedial help available in Math and English. Labs in sciences.
> Microcomputer lab for word processing after school and for elective
> course in Programming. Two language labs per week in French and
> Spanish. Minimal use of audiovisual equipment, field trips, and so
> on.
>
> Administrative: All filing is manual; electric and manual typewriters,
> photocopier; mimeograph in office; two phone lines.
>
> Source: Assistant Principal.

To summarize responses to interviews based on a schedule like the
General Orientation Interview, practitioners may group together
responses to each question that make the same point and then record
each type of response and the number of people giving it. If, for
example, eight employees in a branch of a fast-food chain were interviewed, a typical entry in the summary might read as follows:

> Are there any difficulties and barriers to getting work done here or
> doing it the way you'd like to?
> —annoying customer complaints about food—taste, quality, and so
>   on (3)
> —pressures from supervisor to work faster, come in on weekends (2)
> —none (2)
> —we often run out of buns (1)

Practitioners may choose to present the entire range of responses as
feedback in order to stimulate analysis of the operations and suggestions for their improvement, or they may summarize findings about
organizational strengths and problems in a feedback report. In the
hypothetical case above, if feedback was to be provided to the supervisor, the former method would probably be preferred, so that the two
people who complained about the supervisor would not be singled
out for attention.

The system model itself can also be used to analyze and present data about relationships between elements. A graphic approach that aids both analysis and feedback is to place all eight elements in a circle, list their important subcomponents, and draw color-coded lines between those elements or subcomponents that promote some focal condition, such as job satisfaction, and those that hinder it. Data supporting the inferences in the figure can be recorded separately and used appropriately in feedback.

CHOOSING EFFECTIVENESS CRITERIA

The systems model can also help consultants choose criteria for assessing an organization's current state and develop measures of effectiveness.

Types of Criteria

Output, system state, and adaptation criteria. Table 2 groups the many criteria that have been used to assess organizational effectiveness into three broad categories (see Cameron, 1980; Campbell, 1977; Kanter & Brinkerhoff, 1981). These criteria derive from clients' and consultants' images of some preferred organizational state and from their assumptions about the organizational conditions that can facilitate the achievement of those states. *Output-goal criteria* correspond to many of the specific targets toward which members of organizations strive. Sometimes they are expressed in terms of the success or failure to achieve some end, such as the design of a solar-powered bicycle or a city commission's development of a workable rezoning plan. Criteria dealing with output goals are most appropriate where goals can be defined in terms of clear, measurable objectives and members of the client organization agree about the meaning and importance of these goals. In contrast, this type of criterion is hard to use if members disagree about goals or if goals cannot be readily defined and measured, as is often the case in service and cultural organizations. Even if members of these organizations agree on some abstract goal, such as improving public health, they are likely to differ on its operational meaning and its measurement. An additional drawback of defining effectiveness solely in terms of output goals is that this approach tends to confine the consultant to a technical, evaluator's role.

TABLE 2
Effectiveness Criteria

Type	Operational Definitions
(1) Output Goals	
Goal Attainment	Success/Failure (e.g., rocket launching).
Quantity of Outputs	Productivity (units produced, hours of services provided, values of sales, services—sometimes per work unit or per time period); profits (revenues minus costs); revenues as percentage of investment; percentage of target group reached by services, messages.
Quality of Outputs	Number of rejects, returns, complaints; client, customer satisfaction; expert rating of services (e.g., in health education) or work performance (e.g., in manufacturing, military); impact of services or products on target population (e.g., impact of antilitter campaign).
(2) Internal System State	
Costs of Production or Services	Efficiency (ratio of output value to costs—e.g., labor, equipment—with constant quality); wastage, downtime.
Human Outcomes	Employee satisfactions with pay, working conditions and relationships; motivation (disposition to work); work effort (observed, reported); low absenteeism, lateness, and turnover; health and safety of workforce.
Consensus/Conflict	Agreement on goals and procedures; cohesion (mutual attraction, and identification with work group, and organization); cooperation (reported/observed) within and between units; few strikes, work stoppages, disputes, and feuds.
Work and Information Flows	Smooth flow of products, ideas and information; few snags, foul-ups, misunderstandings; rich, multidirectional communication, accurate analysis of information.

Interpersonal Relations	High levels of trust; open communication of feelings, needs between ranks; de-emphasis of status differences.
Participation	Subordinates participate in making decisions affecting them; diffusion of power and authority.
Fit	Compatibility of requirements of system elements.

(3) *Adaptation and Resource Position*

Resources-quantity	Size of organization (employees; cash, physical assets); resource flows (e.g., investment, grants and budget support in nonprofit organizations).
Resources-quality	Human capital (experience, and training of employees); desirability of clients (e.g., selectiveness of college admissions); reputation of staff.
Legitimacy	Support and approval by community and public bodies; public image; compliance with standards of legal, regulatory, professional bodies (e.g., government pollution control standards, accreditation of college).
Competitive/ Strategic Position	Market share, ranking among competitors in size, volume of business; reputation within the field or industry; full use of capacities to exploit external opportunities.
Impact on Environment	Ability to shape demand, government action, behavior of competitors, suppliers.
Adaptiveness	Adjustment to changes in inputs and demands for outputs; flexibility in handling crises, surprises.
Innovativeness	Number, quality of new products, services, procedures; incorporation of new technologies, management practices.
Fit	Compatibility of internal system elements with requirements, constraints of environment.

Many of the criteria in the second category refer to *internal organizational states and processes* that can contribute to achieving output goals, whereas others, like efficiency or employee satisfaction (see Chapter 3, "Quality of work life outcomes"), are sometimes regarded as ends in themselves. Efficiency and cost-related criteria are hard to apply to nonprofit organizations because of the difficulties of measuring all of the important aspects of outputs and inputs. In contrast, the system criteria relating to internal relationships and processes can be applied to any type of organization. They can be viewed as desirable states or as indicators of some more global state of organizational "health" (e.g., Beckhard, 1969) that facilitates coping with organizational challenges. Criteria relating to internal system states are also useful in the diagnosis of departments or subunits that have little control over their environments.

Many of the *adaptation and resource-position criteria* are applicable to nonprofit organizations, which may have unclear output goals, as well as to commercial firms. Even nonprofit organizations operate as open systems that compete for funds, personnel, and other scarce resources and face pressures to adapt to changing external conditions (see Chapter 5).

Comparison standards. In choosing and developing working definitions of effectiveness, consultants must decide what time frames and comparison standards to use (Cameron, 1980). They may compare

—current and past levels of effectiveness, e.g., rates of growth, development
—the effectiveness of units within the same organization, e.g., comparisons of efficiency ratings, accidents, quality
—the client organization's effectiveness to that of others in the same industry or field, e.g., comparisons of profitability or sales to industry figures
—the organization's current state to some minimum standard, e.g., conformity to federal environmental standards
—the current state to an ideal standard, e.g., innovativeness or community service

The time frame used may vary from hours or days to several years, depending in part on the organizational feature being assessed. Different time frames can also be applied to the same phenomenon. A manufacturing firm's performance may seem impressive, for example, if we look at its current quarterly profits or return on investment. In contrast. if that firm is achieving the results by cutting costs and aggressively marketing current products, it may be unable to sustain these results for more than a year or two because of lack of investment in new product development (Hayes & Abernathy, 1980).

Conflicts among effectiveness criteria. Although all the effectiveness criteria listed in Table 2 may seem reasonable at first glance, there actually are many contradictions and tensions among them. For example, growth usually indicates that an organization is successful in obtaining needed resources, but growth can also lead to less participation in decision making, reduced efficiency, and less ability to adjust to environmental change. The same manager may have conflicting priorities and evaluative criteria without being aware of the conflicts, because the criteria are not evoked simultaneously or their operational implications are not spelled out fully.

An additional problem is that few effectiveness criteria equally suit the interests and priorities of all members of an organization. The many groups and individuals who have a stake in an organization often have conflicting interests and engage in recurrent bargaining and influence struggles to promote their own goals and interests. In pursuing their own purposes, these *stakeholders* (or *constituencies*) typically advocate the use of divergent effectiveness criteria (Pennings & Goodman, 1977). In an industrial firm, for example, stockholders may want more short-term profits, while the research and development people favor investment that will support innovation and growth in the long run, and the unions press for better wages and working conditions. Hence, those effectiveness criteria that best reflect the interests and needs of one subgroup, such as the dominant decision makers within the top management, will probably neglect the priorities of less powerful managers, external clients, production workers, government regulators, and so on.

How to Choose Effectiveness Criteria

If the various effectiveness criteria are not mutually compatible and applicable, how should consultants choose appropriate criteria and incorporate them into diagnosis? To make these decisions they need to consider three sets of questions (Campbell, 1977; Goodman & Pennings, 1980):

(1) Who are the main clients for the study, what do they regard as the preferred state of the organization, and what criteria reflect the

degree of attainment of this state? How can the consultant help them
resolve conflicts and ambiguities among their stated preferences?

(2) What other states or conditions will help promote client goals or are
otherwise appropriate as effectiveness criteria?

(3) How can consultants encourage clients to adopt these additional
priorities?

Identifying clients and clarifying their priorities. The main clients for
a diagnosis are those people who will have responsibility for deciding
what actions (if any) should be taken in light of the diagnostic
findings and for planning and implementing such actions. These
individuals are usually, but not always, the ones who originally
solicited and sponsored the study.

One way for consultants to deal with conflicts between clients and
other stakeholders about effectiveness is to ask clients to develop a
working consensus with guidelines for choosing effectiveness criteria
(e.g., Beckhard & Harris, 1977). Clients can then meet to define their
priorities for the diagnosis with or without the help of the consultant.
If this approach is impractical, consultants may simply accept the
goals and priorities of the most powerful clients and then seek to find
ways of achieving them that will bring benefits to the broadest possible spectrum of members and stakeholders (see Chapter 6, "Who
Benefits?").

Consultants may also press clients to set priorities when the clients
hold ambiguous or internally inconsistent views of what is best for
the organization. To help resolve such conflicts and ambiguities,
consultants should carefully examine data on the priorities reflected
in actual practice (see Chapter 4), rather than relying solely on stated
priorities. For example, consultants can examine how much top
management has invested in research and development and whether
they have recently promoted anyone who bucked the tide to cham-
pion a new product or administrative procedure, rather than relying
on management's declarations of good intentions in these areas.
When practitioners examine the priorities underlying major decisions,
resource allocations, and patterns of rewarding and evaluating performance, they may find that operative goals and priorities diverge
greatly from stated purposes.

If consultants discover major discrepancies between declared and
operative priorities early in a diagnosis, they may present their
findings to clients and help them to rework their priorities and
conceptions of effectiveness in light of the feedback or help clients
redouble their efforts to achieve their initially stated goals. This
process of providing feedback about group goals and priorities can

sometimes become a major focus of intervention that can help clients clarify their goals, priorities, policies, and evaluative criteria. In more client-oriented studies, the process of examining and clarifying priorities can occur quite naturally as consultants and clients collaborate in choosing effectiveness criteria during the design and analysis phases.

Choosing additional criteria. In most diagnoses consultants introduce additional effectiveness criteria that do not derive directly from initial client priorities but point to conditions (such as teamwork or flexibility) that can contribute to the achievement of clients' goals or are generally compatible with the clients' image of the desired state of the organization. Sometimes consultants also lead clients toward a radically different image of what is good for their organization—for example, by suggesting that if the organization does not become more innovative, it will ultimately encounter problems of adapting to its environment.

By introducing effectiveness criteria relating to the organization's internal system state and to its ability to obtain resources and adapt to its environment (see Table 2), practitioners can often help their clients redefine specific problems and challenges in terms of needs for improving broader, underlying forms of effectiveness. If these broader aspects of effectiveness can be enhanced, the organization will be better able to handle future problems, as well as coping with current ones. For example, enhancing the satisfaction and motivation of workers can help reduce such immediate symptoms of dissatisfaction as rapid employee turnover, absenteeism, and noncompliance with minimal performance requirements. But improving quality of work life, satisfaction, and motivation can also yield long-term benefits, such as a loyal, flexible work force.

In like manner, the criteria related to smooth, cooperative internal relationships and processes need not be applied only in cases of rancorous conflict or poor work flow. They are appropriate whenever work requires high levels of mutual consultation and cooperation—for instance, in professional and administrative teams. The major drawback of criteria that assume the need for fits among system parts and for smooth, trustful relations among employees is that they may lead practitioners to underestimate the potential contribution of tension and conflict to organizational change and adaptation. Conflict may be too low rather than too high if work standards are lax, if members automatically submit to authority, or if they avoid confronting the challenges and problems facing their organization (Robbins, 1978).

Criteria relating to resource position and adaptation are especially relevant when the task environment is changing very rapidly (e.g., in high-technology industries), is highly competitive, or poses a serious challenge to the client organization's viability (e.g., in social services faced with budget cuts). These criteria are especially suited for work with high-level administrators who have both the authority and the willingness to work for change in their organization's (or their division's) relation to its environment.

Clients are likely to reject findings that reflect priorities and evaluative standards that they do not understand or with which they disagree. Hence, consultants should reach an understanding with clients as soon as possible after agreeing to conduct a diagnosis about the effectiveness criteria, time frames, and comparison standards that will be used.

Problems of Measuring Effectiveness

In principle, the procedure for developing systematic measures of effectiveness is identical to that of developing any kind of measure (e.g., Selltiz et al., 1981). After clarifying the concept conceptually, the investigator specifies concretely what phenomena will be considered indicative of effectiveness and chooses measures that fit this operational definition. Here is an example that shows how the initial conceptualization of effectiveness affects subsequent choices:

Conceptualization A: Effectiveness refers (in part) to the absence of rancorous conflict among the people and groups who contribute to work flow
  Operational definition: absence of conflicts that interrupt work flow
  Possible measures: number of days lost to strikes and number of work stoppages
Conceptualization B: Effectiveness refers to smooth work flow
  Operational definition: absence of all types of interruptions in the work flow
  Possible measures: amount of time that units are idle while waiting for inputs; number of interruptions; total time to produce a product or complete some operation (e.g., develop marketing plan)

In practice, consultants may have to define and measure effectiveness in ways that allow them to engage in secondary analysis of data that are available or can be gathered quickly and inexpensively. Unless they keep clear conceptual and operational definitions of effectiveness in mind when working with these less-than-perfect data, they may interpret their findings incorrectly and overlook important phenomena that are not covered by these measures. For example, data on pupils' performance on standardized achievement tests might be readily available to consultants conducting a diagnosis of an elementary school. Unfortunately, these tests do not measure many important educational outcomes, such as the ability to engage in self study, critical thinking, and creativity. Yet these kinds of outcomes and the social and educational processes occurring within the school may actually be more relevant to the diagnosis than the outcomes on which data are available. A further problem arises when data were originally designed to evaluate the performance of employees or units. In such cases, members may have learned to perform in ways that make them look good on the measured criteria, such as the number of sales completed, while neglecting other desirable forms of behavior—such as customer satisfaction or service—that are less closely monitored (Lawler & Rhode, 1976).

Another issue in measuring effectiveness is the value of using objective, behavioral measures of effectiveness (such as the number of strike days), as opposed to subjective measures reflecting the judgements of participants of experts (e.g., descriptions of the quality of labor relations in the plant). In practice, this distinction often turns out to be far from clear cut (Campbell, 1977, p. 45). For example, the number of units manufactured in a plant during a month is apparently an objective measure, but we must have a standard in order to decide whether the figure is too high, too low, or just right. Even comparing the figure to past performance does not resolve the problem. Is a 5% growth over last year substantial or lackluster, in light of the efforts and investments made? In the final analysis, the kinds of objective data that managers collect and pay attention to and their evaluations of these figures all depend heavily on their subjective priorities and standards.

ASSESSING THE FEASIBILITY OF CHANGE
AND CHOOSING APPROPRIATE INTERVENTIONS

Interpretive and Process Issues

Consultants need to consider the following issues during diagnosis in order to decide what steps, if any, will help clients solve problems and enhance organizational effectiveness (see also Burke, 1982, pp. 215–233; President et al., 1980):

(1) Does the organization need basic changes? When performance gaps and other signs of ineffectiveness show up in diagnoses, consultants and clients should decide whether small system adjustments or basic changes are needed and then choose feasible routes toward either form of improvement. The periodic adjustments in procedures that most organizations use to cope with surprises and environmental fluctuations are typical of small *system adjustments* that do not fundamentally alter any system elements. Retailers, for example, temporarily hire extra help during the Christmas rush, and most organizations go through troubleshooting episodes during which members drop everyday matters and devote themselves to meeting a deadline or resolving a crisis. In like manner, managers may adjust rules and standard operating procedures slightly to cope with problems without making any fundamental changes.

In contrast, *basic changes* such as structural reorganizations (e.g., eliminating or creating positions), processual changes (e.g., increasing participation in decision making), and technological changes (e.g., computerizing record-keeping) substantially alter practices within one or more system elements and often have consequences that are felt at many organizational levels and within many systems elements. Such changes often reflect revised goals, strategies, and plans and usually require difficult decisions about reallocating funds and other resources.

Basic changes are needed when current ways of shifting routines and procedures to cope with problems have become insufficient or are likely to become outmoded in the near future. Troubleshooting procedures and other system adjustments are inadequate if an organization has fallen into a state of permanent crisis, lurching from one troubleshooting episode to another, or if the short-term solutions to crises create long-lasting havoc in the organization (Sayles, 1979, pp. 160–162). Moreover, basic changes are probably needed if symptoms of ineffectiveness such as quality problems, operating inefficiencies, and low morale persist despite many efforts to use "quick and easy" techniques to deal with these problems.

(2) Is there readiness for change? Members of an organization and external stakeholders often realize that "something must be done" to change an organization when they are faced with mounting signs of ineffectiveness—such as declining sales, poor quality, eroding budget support, labor unrest, internal conflict, or failures to exploit opportunities—or when they adopt new goals and strategies that call for

changes like growth, diversification, and innovation. Such shifts in priorities can occur as a result of changes in management or in response to the example of other organizations that pioneer a new technique, like robotics, or create new opportunities (e.g., by creating a new market). Diagnostic feedback that shows clients and other members that organizational problems are more acute or more widespread than they had thought may also increase readiness for change *if* the recipients of the feedback are not threatened by the prospect of change.

(3) How will members and external stakeholders react to proposed interventions? In considering possible steps to improve effectiveness, consultants need to consider whether clients, other members, and external stakeholders are likely to cooperate with an intervention or resist it. In particular, during diagnosis consultants should try to determine whether key decision makers and other powerful groups (see Chapter 4) are likely to support particular interventions and provide the backing and resources needed to implement them successfully. They should also examine the extent to which possible interventions are likely to encounter resistance because they threaten people's power, prestige, job security, or other interests. Typical sources of resistance include

—community groups that oppose institutional expansion into residential neighborhoods
—regulatory bodies that require evidence that new programs or products meet environmental, equal opportunity, or safety standards
—managers who are skeptical about the efficacy of an unfamiliar intervention, like the introduction of flexible working hours, and worried about its costs
—unions and employees who fight proposals for redefining job responsibilities, consolidating jobs or units, or rolling back wages
—people whose prestige or power depends on current procedures or arrangements
—managers who fear that sensitivity training or other process interventions will pry into their personal lives and feelings.

If diagnosis suggests that a particular form of intervention may encounter serious resistance by clients, members, or outside stakeholders, then consultants should try to find other steps toward improvement that are less threatening and better fit the expressed needs and concerns of these groups, rather than trying to expose and confront resistance (Harrison, 1970). They might, for example, suggest that management consider retraining and relocating employees whose jobs would be eliminated by merging two divisions, rather than firing them.

(4) Does the organization have the capacity to implement the changes? Even if there is no active resistance to a proposed intervention, the client organization may not have the capacity to make these changes. To assess the capacity to make particular change, practitioners can check whether each system element can be expected to make the contributions required for the change to be made successfully. To make this assessment consultants can ask themselves questions such as these:

—Does the organization have the resources—people, funds, talent, knowledge, etc.—and technology needed to make the change or can it obtain them?
—Can current structural and technical arrangements be adapted to accommodate and facilitate the change?
—Will dominant behavior patterns, processes, beliefs, and values (culture) support the new kinds of behavior that the change will introduce?
—Will the environment provide the necessary support, permission, and resources to make the change feasible?

In assessing capacity, practitioners make judgments about the probable fit between current practices and proposed changes (see Chapter 4 "Diagnosing System Fits"). For example, when Sears Roebuck decided to offer a wide range of financial services such as insurance, personal loans, and automatic teller machines, observers (e.g., Business Week, 1981b) questioned whether its managers, who were steeped in the culture of mass-market retailing, could learn to adapt to the business style of the insurance and financial services industries. In addition, the question was raised whether the divergent retailing and financial services operations could successfully be integrated within a single organizational structure.

(5) Will the proposed changes achieve the desired results without having undesirable consequences? Before recommending changes, practitioners should make a final accounting of the probable benefits and risks of each possible intervention. By considering the likely impacts of proposed changes on all system elements and on the interactions among them, consultants may check whether the change is likely to have the desired consequences without creating other, unintended consequences that would undercut its benefits. Interventions are more likely to succeed if they fit the conditions in the client organization, including:

—members' characteristics (e.g., preferences for pay versus more vacation time)

—organizational and technical conditions (e.g., equipment, division of labor)

—external constraints (e.g., consumer preferences)

—organizational culture (informal norms, values, and beliefs)

In the case of 21C Scientific Instruments (see Chapter 1), for example, the consultant sought to tap the talents of division managers and help the firm move from a paternalistic management style that rewarded loyalty to the firm toward a more performance-oriented style. To do so the consultant might have proposed increasing the authority and autonomy of division managers. But this intervention could have had very undesirable consequences: Pressures by division managers for greater efficiency and productivity and the firing or relocation of veteran employees would have created shock and hostility among remaining employees, who were accustomed to job security and limited pressure for performance. These developments could have led to low morale, labor unrest, and conflict between managers attached to the old, paternalistic style of management and those who championed expanding and streamlining operations—no matter what the costs for current employees.

Consultants should weigh the likely positive and negative effects of any interventions that might produce *lasting* improvements in effectiveness. Then they can recommend the beneficial interventions that are least likely to encounter serious resistance or have other undesirable consequences and that require the lowest levels of support and commitment from members (see Harrison, 1970). If these steps succeed, more ambitious interventions can be considered subsequently.

Methodological Issues

Assessing support and resistance to change. In examining readiness for change and the likely consequences of implementing some change, practitioners should bear in mind that people's attitudes toward a proposal are not very good predictors of how they will behave if it is actually implemented (see Fishbein & Ajzen, 1975, on the difficulty of predicting behavior from attitudes). Social pressures from peers or supervisors may make people hesitate to reveal their true feelings. Moreover, after change has occurred, members may change their attitudes as they discover that its costs and benefits differ greatly from what they anticipated. Despite these drawbacks, attitudinal data may reveal previously unnoticed hostility toward proposed changes. In addition, interviews with powerful individuals, including influential leaders who lack formal authority, may indicate whether they will support or resist an intervention.

Because of the difficulty of predicting people's actions from their attitudes, consultants seeking to assess readiness for change and its likely consequences should also examine the ways in which members reacted in the past when changes were introduced. If practitioners and clients carefully consider the specific nature of past interventions and the ways in which they were introduced, they may be able to discover the most feasible types of changes and the best procedures for introducing them.

Testing for capacity, readiness, and consequences. The complexity of organizational relations and the indeterminacy of future behavior make it very difficult to anticipate peoples' reactions to change and the consequences of particular interventions. As a result, consultants and managers sometimes take a more experimental approach to implementation. They may, for instance, implement a change in stages, beginning with some preliminary activity (such as an off-site meeting with top managers to plan changes) in order to learn from members' reaction to each stage how they may react to subsequent stages. By developing contingency plans for responding to possible developments at each stage, consultants can prepare to recommend appropriate steps to implementation.

Another variation on this approach is to introduce an intervention as an experiment in one or more units within an organization. After a period of running-in and an assessment of the consequences, the innovation can be modified in light of this experience and then diffused to other parts of the organization. Managers often take this approach when introducing costly technological changes or introducing structural changes, such as job enrichment, in which routine jobs are made more complex and challenging. Unfortunately, managers in both the public and private sectors sometimes agree to introduce such a pilot program in order to show that they are forward looking, although, in fact, they have little intention of extending the program to the rest of the organization. An additional drawback to experimental programs is that the enthusiasm created by the newness and uniqueness of the program may be lost when the change is introduced widely and becomes well established.

EXERCISES

1. Effectiveness Criteria

Conduct an open, semistructured interview with one of the people in charge of an organization (or unit) to which you have access. First ask the person to describe an example of successful operations in the organization. Then ask in general what the objectives are toward which the organization should strive and how they know whether they are achieving them. Based on these responses and any other data you have (e.g., impressions from the previous exercise),

(1) specify the effectiveness criteria to which the respondent referred;
(2) explain whether these criteria reflect considerations of output, system state, or adaptation;
(3) suggest additional effectiveness criteria that would fit the expressed priorities and needs of those in charge of the organization;
(4) note criteria that would reflect the interests of other internal and outside stakeholders.

2. Resistance to Change

Talk with a manager or organizational authority who can describe the individuals and groups within the organization and those outside of it that have a stake in the decisions made by its top management. Then ask the manager to describe how these stakeholders would react to a particular change—some step that the manager thinks might help solve a problem or enhance effectiveness. Organize your data in a chart with a column for the stakeholders likely to support this change or cooperate with it and a column for those likely to resist it. In parentheses rank each group as strong, moderate, or weak in terms of its impact on the organization. Write a summary describing your interview, the current balance of forces supporting the change and opposing it, and the kinds of steps toward improvement that seem feasible in light of the forces shown in your table.

3. General Orientation Interviews

Plan a General Orientation Interview (see Appendix A) that concentrates on the specific unit (e.g., department) in which the person being interviewed works. Note in advance which questions are inappropriate and will be skipped (e.g., Section V) and which will need rewording to make them more applicable. Do not spend more than an hour on this first interview, even if you cannot cover all questions. Write a report in which you summarize the problems you encountered in conducting the interview (e.g., keeping the respondent on track, time pressures, skipping questions concerning areas with which the respondent was unfamiliar). Explain how you would handle the next interview. After getting feedback on your report from your instructor, conduct two more interviews with members of the same or similar units and summarize the findings to all three interviews in terms of the headings provided in Appendix A (e.g., "The Person and His or Her Job. . .").

3

Assessing Performance-Related Behavior and the Quality of Work Life

A model is provided to guide the diagnosis of factors affecting individual and group performance and the quality of work life. Techniques for gathering, analyzing, and feeding back data are also examined. Special attention is given to standardized questionnaires and to techniques for observing group processes. Broader issues of method, interpretation, and process are also considered.

"The pace and quality of work in the department are lackluster."

"We are losing our top staff people, but the less promising ones stay on."

"Our weekly program-review meetings have deteriorated to the point where we argue repeatedly about the same issues and never get anywhere."

"How can we make the clerical work less boring and more appealing?"

These statements illustrate typical problems that potential clients —who are usually managers but may also include employee representatives—might present to consultants. As the presented problems involve individual and group-level issues, consultants might reasonably begin the diagnosis at these levels. Depending on the findings, the redefined problem that emerged during the diagnosis might remain at the individual or group levels, or it might include divisional or even organizationwide features.

A MODEL FOR DIAGNOSING
INDIVIDUAL AND GROUP BEHAVIOR

To analyze individual and group-level phenomena, practitioners need a guiding model that shows the important factors to examine and points to the relationships among them. The model shown in

Figure 2, which builds on the open-system model (Figure 1), specifies the individual and group-level factors that a broad diagnosis would encompass.[1] More focused diagnostic studies would consider only a subset of factors that were found to be important during scouting and were closely related to client concerns. The model in Figure 2 assumes that group and organizational contexts greatly affect individual behavior and that group behavior and processes are likewise influenced by the larger organizational context. Hence, the components are shown at three levels—the total organization, the group, and the individual. Lower-level phenomena (such as individual attitudes and beliefs) can also have significant effects on higher-level ones—such as group actions and norms—as is shown in Figure 2 by the arrows that are directed upward and by the dotted feedback loops. For simplicity the model does not distinguish between division and organization-level phenomena, but this distinction may be important if divisions differ substantially from one another. All of the components in Figure 2 are surrounded by broken lines to show their openness to environmental influences like these:

—Prevailing norms and attitudes in the environment affect employees' assumptions about the fairness of job requirements (e.g., travel) and personnel policies (e.g., paid personal leave days).
—The state of labor markets affects the ease with which discontented employees can leave the organization.
—External groups, such as unions and regulatory agencies, affect technologies and administrative procedures (e.g., by requiring the advertisement of job openings).

Let us look briefly at each of the major components of the model.

Outputs

Group performance. Clients often turn to consultants for help with performance-related problems such as poor quality of goods and services produced, low productivity, high costs, interruptions and delays in work flows, and the failure of groups to act aggressively (e.g., poor sales performance) or creatively (e.g., outmoded marketing

---

1. Figure 2 and the following discussion draw in part on Lawler et al. (1983, pp. 20–25) but expand that discussion considerably. Readers who are unfamiliar with the field of organizational behavior will probably want to consult a recent text in the field (e.g., Gordon, 1983) and the references cited in this chapter before conducting a diagnosis.

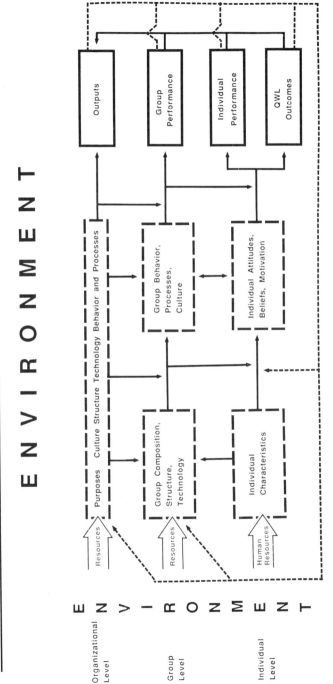

NOTE: Solid lines show main lines of influence; dotted lines show feeback loops.

Figure 2: A Model for Diagnosing Individual and Group Behavior

campaigns). To assess group functioning in terms of outputs, consultants need to define the goods or services produced by the group. In management groups these outputs often consist of solutions to problems (e.g. how to increase market share), plans, tactics, and procedures for coordinating the work of other units.

Individual performance-related behavior. This category includes the degree and quality of members' efforts, their degree of initiative, cooperation with other employees, levels of absenteeism, lateness, and commitment to the job—as opposed to attempts to leave the organization or move within it in ways that do not fit accepted career lines. The important aspects of performance will depend on the group's tasks, goals, and standards. In a surveyor's team within a city agency, for example, accuracy and reliability may be more highly valued than the speed with which the work is done.

Quality of work life (QWL) outcomes. Quality of working life refers to the degree to which the work in an organization contributes to the material and psychological well-being of its members. Diagnostic studies often assess QWL in terms of employees' levels of satisfaction with the following conditions:

—job security
—fairness and adequacy of pay
—working conditions
—interpersonal relations
—meaningfulness and challenge of work

It is also possible to obtain descriptions of QWL conditions from employees or to have independent observers rate QWL conditions. QWL studies can also examine objective and subjective indicators of physical and mental health, including the amount of stress experienced at work (e.g., Kets de Vries, 1979).

For many years consultants and researchers assumed that improving QWL would inevitably heighten employee motivation and would thereby enhance job performance and productivity. Today it is recognized that enhancing employee motivation and QWL can enhance performance under some conditions but not others (e.g., Walton, 1975). Pressures to increase productivity, for example, can reduce job safety or security, and improvements in working conditions may raise costs without showing up in "bottom line" improvements in productivity or revenues. Still, improving QWL can contribute directly to reducing turnover and absenteeism and in the long run may help create a well-trained, loyal work force that is more willing and able to adapt to change. Moreover, QWL outcomes are increasingly accepted as desirable ends in their own right. Academics and unions have been among the leaders in the QWL movement (e.g., Davis & Cherns, 1975), but some business leaders have also endorsed this trend (e.g., Business Week, 1981a).

Factors Affecting Performance and QWL

Individual characteristics. Table 3 summarizes the individual-level factors that research suggests can affect performance and QWL. Because a wide range of conditions may influence the impacts of these factors, practitioners should investigate their effects in the client organization, rather than assuming that these effects are identical to those observed in other organizations. The traits and characteristics listed in the first part of the table can all have a direct bearing on the motivation of employees to perform a task and their ability to do so. These characteristics become particularly important for organizational diagnosis when they are shared by sizable groups of employees. Suppose, for example, that the sales department of an insurance company was having difficulty attracting top college graduates even though the firm offered marginally higher commissions than its competitors. Taking into account the needs that probably characterize college graduates who are considering a career in insurance, a consultant might suggest that the department try offering recruits a chance to learn about the entire insurance business rather than just using monetary incentives to attract good candidates.

Sometimes practitioners can trace changes in employees' motivations, in their perceptions about rewards, and in group processes and behavior to shifting work force characteristics. The rise in the educational level of blue-collar employees, for example, has led to greater demands by factory workers for interesting, challenging work. Despite the importance of individual and work force characteristics like these, practitioners should be cautioned that members of an organization sometimes overestimate the importance of personal traits. They may assume, for example, that all the problems of a failing program or department could be solved, if only the "right person" could be found to run it or the right staff members were chosen. When a unit's problems seem likely to persist even if the "ideal" manager is found, then group and organizational causes should be considered, rather than personal ones

Individual attitudes, beliefs, and motivations. The second part of Table 3 lists attitudes and orientations that can affect performance and that reflect QWL. Motivation and satisfactions with rewards have repeatedly been shown to affect *job commitment* which often shows up in attendance and low turnover. Job satisfaction is also

TABLE 3
Key Individual Factors

Individual Characteristics

Physical and mental state—health, abilities, job-related traits (e.g.,
    pleasant voice for switchboard operator).
Social background and traits—sex, age, ethnic, and regional back-
    ground.
Training and education—formal education, technical training, work
    experience.
Individual needs—importance of various types of rewards, work
    conditions (e.g., job security versus high pay—see Hackman &
    Oldham, 1980; Salancik & Pfeffer, 1977).*

Individual Attitudes, Beliefs, Motivation

Motivation—to work well, to remain in the job.
Rewards experienced
    —extrinsic: pay, benefits, promotion possibilities, peer approval,
        social status, nonmonetary compensation (e.g., flexible hours,
        opportunities for training), physical conditions, location,
        security.
    —intrinsic: personal growth, learning, interest, feeling of accom-
        plishment (Lawler, 1977).
Job felt to be intrinsically rewarding—job is meaningful; employee is
    responsible for important results, gets feedback on work, and sees
    its results (Hackman & Oldham, 1980).
Expectations
    —link between job performance and valued rewards (e.g., If you
        run project well, will get promotion—see Lawler, 1977).
    —consequences of personal effort, initiative, innovation (e.g., What
        happens to people who find new ways of doing things?).
    —ability to get things done (Kanter 1977).
Equity—feeling that efforts are fairly rewarded (Goodman, 1977).
Trust—ability to rely on, believe peers, managers (Schein, 1969).
Specific attitudes—satisfaction with current procedures (e.g., grievance
    procedures); attitudes, evaluations of group and specific projects
    (e.g., customer relations campaign—Nadler, et al., 1976); attitudes
    toward proposed changes (e.g., early retirement proposal).

*References are to chapters in this book and useful sources.

associated with other aspects of performance, although the causal relations between these variables are complex. By examining employee's *expectations*, consultants may discover additional explanations for suboptimal performance. If, for example, employees in a busy city hotel are convinced that nothing can be done to make disgruntled guests more satisfied with the service, they are unlikely to improve the situation. In addition, if employees expect their efforts to improve performance to go unrewarded or to result in rewards that are not important to them (e.g., citation for service in the chain's newsletter), they will remain unmotivated to act.

Diagnoses can also benefit from the assessment of attitudes and beliefs that are directly related to questions being debated within an organization. Members may be asked, for example, how they feel about specific proposals and policies such as the proposed introduction of a new personnel policy (but see Chapter 2, "Assessing . . . resistance to change"). Repeated attitude surveys can also provide feedback on particular programs or groups. This information can then contribute to the assessment of progress toward a stated goal and can help managers spot problems before they become critical (e.g., Nadler et al., 1976).

Group composition, structure, and technology Table 4 lists and illustrates some of the major group-level factors referred to in Figure 2. As the table indicates, group behavior can be shaped by the proportions and composition of groups as well as the characteristics of their members. When women or members of an ethnic group are in the minority in management, for example, they may feel pressures to overachieve or to minimize their visibility (Kanter, 1977). Divergences in social background, work experience, and professional training can also lead to conflicts about how work should be conducted and about values and goals. Such conflicts are very common in interdisciplinary teams in the human services and in management teams that draw their members from divergent functional specializations, such as marketing and production.

The behavior of group members is also shaped by the structural and technological factors listed in Table 4. By examining them carefully consultants can sometimes find sources of ineffective behavior and discover ways to change this behavior (see Chapter 4). For example, the controls used to monitor performance and the standards for evaluating it can sometimes encourage behavior that management considers undesirable while discouraging other, desired forms of behavior. In most universities, for instance, faculty are encouraged to devote themselves more to research than to teaching

TABLE 4
Key Group Factors

Group Composition, Structure, and Technology

Social and Occupational Composition—Mix of members' social and
personal characteristics (e.g., Americans versus locals in overseas
office); proportions of minorities; divergence of professional training and work experience (e.g., veteran managers versus new
MBAs).

Structure—nature, extent of rules and work procedures (e.g., reliance
on judgment, intuition versus rules, past precedents); flexibility,
clarity of task assignments, responsibilities, accountability
(Chapter 4); degree of autonomy of members (How much say do
they have over work procedures and assignments?) (Chapter 4);
types of controls (e.g., reports, direct supervision, computer
monitoring of output; evaluation by outsiders; see also, Van De
Ven & Ferry, 1980, pp. 155–187); frequency, comprehensiveness of
controls (Are all important processes and outcomes monitored or
only some?); coordination mechanisms (e.g., meetings, supervision, committees, teams—see Chapter 4).

Technology—impact of work procedures and physical arrangements
on group processes (e.g., noise prevents conversation, layout inhib-
its group work; see also Pasmore & Sherwood, 1978); types of
work-flow interdependencies (Chapter 4); motivational potential of
job (e.g., repetition, challenge; see also Hackman & Oldham, 1980).

Group Behavior, Processes, and Culture

Relationships among Group Members—cohesiveness (feelings of
attachment to group; similarity of views, behavior).

Processes:

—Rewarding: types of behavior rewarded (e.g., conformity versus
individual initiative), frequency, consistency, processes of
delivering rewards;

—Communication: direction of information flows (e.g., downward,
horizontally), openness and honesty (e.g., Do members share
problems and issues or try to manipulate one another and keep
themselves "looking good"?)

—Cooperation and conflict—sources, extent, nature; conflict
management (collaboration in search of solution satisfying all
parties, bargaining, forcing of solution by supervisor); impacts of
conflict and conflict management (Robbins, 1978);

—Decision making (methods, participation),

—Problem solving (methods, confrontation versus avoidance).

Supervisory Behavior—Supportiveness (encourages learning, provides help, resources); participativeness (sharing of information and decision making); degree of emphasis on group tasks, objectives (stresses achievement of goals, common purposes); levels and nature of performance expectations (e.g., effort, quality expected); communication and conflict management styles (see Processes).

Culture—Group identity (Do language, shared rituals affirm identity? e.g., talk of "we versus them," marking of significant group events); degree of consensus, clarity about goals, objectives; trust, confidence in peers, managers; expectations about work and rewards (e.g., views on getting ahead, risk taking, cooperation); views on problems, challenges (nature of problems, realism of views); compatibility of group norms with managerial expectations (Chapter 4).

---

because their publications are monitored and evaluated carefully, whereas their teaching performance receives little attention.

The work technology can affect the degree to which jobs are motivating and the kinds of contacts members have with one another (e.g., by influencing how work is coordinated—see Chapter 4, "Fits between work flow . . . "). Many of the structural characteristics listed in the table are discussed in Chapter 4, where research is reviewed showing that people with advanced training in their professions and others who seek challenging jobs prefer to work in units that grant them more autonomy and assign tasks and responsibilities more flexibly.

Group behavior, processes, and culture. Many of the factors in the second part of Table 4 have been treated as keys to organizational effectiveness (see Chapter 2) by organization development consultants (e.g., Beckhard, 1969; Schein, 1969) and applied researchers who draw on the human relations school of organizational behavior (e.g., Likert, 1967; McGregor, 1960). These practitioners argue that the motivations and work efforts of individuals and groups improve when work relations are cooperative and cohesive, communication is honest and multidirectional, group norms support productivity, and decision making is participative. The group supervisor can encourage the development of such a team spirit by sharing information with group members (e.g., by explaining the logic behind new production targets), encouraging participation in decisions directly affecting members, supporting individual effort and learning, facilitating and directing work, and setting high standards for the group. Moving groups toward this ideal is not a panacea for all organizational problems, nor do such groups always achieve higher levels of outputs. However, members of groups like these are usually more satisfied with work, enjoy a higher QWL, and are more committed to the job and the work group (Strauss, 1977). Moreover, groups having these characteristics are often better able to handle tasks involving non-routine problems and calling for creativity and innovation (see Chapter 4, "Organic versus mechanistic structures").

Participative work groups can also enhance productivity and QWL in routine production and service tasks (Strauss, 1982). The *quality circle* movement (e.g., Ouchi, 1981, pp. 261–268), in which workers are given opportunities to make decisions about how to organize and improve their work, is the most recent attempt to use participative methods to improve performance. These participative programs can succeed only if workers and management cooperate, if job security is not threatened, and if employees gain more influence over working conditions and work-related decisions. Otherwise, employees will quickly become cynical about the intentions of management and will stop trying to contribute to decision making (Kanter, 1977).

Organizational factors. There are many links between organization-level factors and those at the group and individual levels that can profitably be explored during diagnosis (see Figure 2 and Chapter 4). First, standards and objectives set by top management (e.g., "Improve market share by 5% during the next quarter") can define the targets that lower-level managers use to evaluate group performance (e.g., "Sell 1000 more units in Tulsa by November"). Moreover, by defining the mission, strategies, and goals of the organization top management can focus individual and group efforts around shared objectives and create expectations about the kinds of behavior that will be rewarded (e.g., "We will go for clients who want full services, not cut-rate deals"). Second as was suggested by the example of faculty evaluation in universities, procedures for monitoring and controlling operations can directly affect group norms (e.g., "Don't spend too much time preparing classes or meeting students"), working styles ("Avoid hanging around the department—stay home and write!"), and output objectives (e.g., "Publish research papers").

Third, such aspects of the organizational culture as widely shared beliefs about the way work gets done, how change occurs, and who has influence also shape individual and group behavior (Argyris &

Schon, 1978; Davis, 1984). Fourth, organizational technology and structure shape coordination and control within groups, the division of labor within and between groups, and the nature of individual-level tasks. If, for example, the members of a law firm are all given personal computers, their needs for secretarial and other supporting services may change radically. They may begin to type memos and make small revisions of contract drafts on their own, thus reducing the need for dictation and routine typing services and changing their working relations with secretaries.

DIAGNOSTIC METHODS AND PROCEDURES

The section that follows examines the design and administration of a diagnosis of individual and group performance and QWL. It also notes some general issues that arise in most diagnoses, no matter what questions or organizational levels are emphasized.

Study Design

Deciding what to study. As suggested above, consultants usually select the topics for study in response to their clients' initial presentations of problems and in keeping with the preliminary diagnosis made during scouting. For instance, the complaint about the argument-ridden, unproductive meetings cited at the beginning of the chapter might lead a consultant to explore the background to the arguments that are plaguing the meetings. Preliminary conversations with participants about their work might reveal major disagreements about program goals and members' responsibilities, along with a lack of mechanisms for working out such difficulties. In keeping with these findings the consultant might decide to examine these group processes and structures more closely.

The choice of diagnostic topics also reflects the effectiveness criteria to be used in assessing individual and group behavior (see Chapter 2). In addition to the output criteria reviewed above, many of the system state criteria listed in Table 2 and developed in Table 4 can also be used as standards for evaluating work groups. Rancorous conflict, for example, is often taken as a sign of group ineffectiveness. The adaptation and resource position criteria in Table 2 can also be applied to small groups if the group's environment is defined as including other units within the larger organization along with salient features of the organization's environment.

Having chosen a particular focus for diagnosis, the practitioner must define carefully the specific factors to be studied and decide on the best way to obtain data on them. To start, practitioners can gather Basic Organizational Information and conduct a limited number of General Orientation Interviews (see Appendix A). Then additional data-gathering steps can be designed as needed. If, for example, the consultant wanted to examine methods for resolving conflicts and solving group problems, he or she could interview group members, paying particular attention to the kinds of issues that create conflicts and the ways they and their supervisors deal with these conflicts. These data might then be supplemented with observations of group meetings. Whether a broad or a narrow focus seems best, practitioners should choose data-gathering methods that are most likely to yield useful, valid results and that will contribute to a positive relationship to clients and other members of the organization (see Chapter 1). Practitioners should avoid relying on some familiar "off-the-shelf" technique like a standard attitude survey when these techniques are inappropriate to the diagnostic questions or will detract from the client-consultant relationship.

Sampling. The data should be as representative as possible of the individuals, groups, and situations under study. For example, to find out about the characteristic ways in which conflicts are handled, the practitioner should try to be sure that the instances of conflict management reported in interviews are typical or representative, as well as ensuring that a cross section of group members are interviewed. To reach large numbers of people, self-administered questionnaires can be distributed to samples of members selected through probability sampling (see Selltiz et al., 1981). Probability samples can also be used to gather secondary data, such as absenteeism rates, from large data sets. Probability sampling is rarely used to choose subjects for interviewing because of the high cost of conducting a large number of interviews. When small groups are to be interviewed or given questionnaires, all members may be included or a cross section of individuals can be selected who are likely to hold different perspectives and points of view.

Sampling issues also arise when observational techniques are used. Because large amounts of time and trained observers are needed, consultants usually prefer to observe important meetings, training sessions, or crucial work activities in which members interact intensively and many aspects of group relations can be seen at the same time. It is best to choose settings for observation that are as central to group operations as possible because behavior can vary greatly from one context (e.g., headquarters) to another (e.g., field operations). Practitioners should also be aware that a unit may operate differently when it convenes as a whole than when its members work alone or in subgroups.

In designing samples, practitioners should take into account the attitudes of group members toward the study and uses to which the data will be put, as well as strictly methodological considerations. If, for example, all members of a large division will receive feedback from a questionnaire about their departments' operations, it may be better to include everyone in the survey. By doing so consultants may increase interest in the questionnaire study and enhance the believ-ability of the feedback.

Administering the study. The procedures used to gather, store, and analyze the data should also be chosen so that they promote a sound consulting relationship, as well as providing valid diagnostic data.[2] Practitioners should make it clear to members of a client organiza-tion that they will store and process the data in a professional fashion and maintain the confidentiality of participants. Moreover, they should explain that only group-level results will be reported, so as to preserve the anonymity of individual members.

Measurement and Data-Gathering Techniques

A combination of data-gathering techniques (see Chapter 1) should usually be used in the diagnosis of performance-related behavior and QWL. The discussion that follows emphasizes the use of questionnaires because of their popularity and appropriateness to the individual and group levels of analysis. It also illustrates the use of observational techniques that are particularly well suited to the study of group processes.

Secondary analysis. In many organizations data on the social or personal characteristics of work group members can be extracted from personnel files using standard procedures for content analysis (see Selltiz et al., 1981). Most organizations also have records of group outputs like sales, productivity, production quality (e.g., percentage of

---

2. For excellent discussions of the methods and procedures of conducting diagnos-tic surveys see Nadler (1977) and Bowditch & Buono (1982).

products serviced under warranty), and services delivered (e.g., number of outpatient visits to a hospital clinic). Organizational publications and records may also provide information on processes, structures, technologies, and purposes, but this information will be hard to code and quantify. These documentary data almost always need to be supplemented with information on actual practices, as opposed to managerial descriptions and declarations (see Chapter 4).

Practitioners who conduct secondary analyses of organizational documents or records need to be aware that these sources reflect the perspectives of the people who gathered the information and the particular reasons for which it was originally gathered. Employee evaluations that were originally used in decisions about raises, for example, may reflect the pressures supervisors felt to present their subordinates in a favorable light. In contrast, negative comments about these employees by more senior managers may reflect their desire to avoid granting raises automatically. Both views are worth examining in order to understand the many ways in which people interpret employee behavior and the factors shaping their interpretations, but neither can be accepted as unbiased.

Interviews. Much diagnostic information about the factors discussed earlier in the chapter can be obtained through General Orientation Interviews (Appendix A) and through interviews that focus more explicitly on individual and group factors. Department heads may provide basic information on their departments and work groups within them, but they are likely to be reluctant to report candidly on actual processes and behavior that may reflect badly upon their performance as managers. In such cases, interviews will be needed with additional department members.

By conducting detailed interviews with members from different backgrounds and locations within a unit and by listening carefully to their accounts of important issues, investigators can become aware of members' distinctive perspectives and viewpoints. For example, department heads may characterize their organization as dealing honestly and directly with employee grievances, whereas subordinates complain that their grievances are ignored or minimized by management. When such divergences seem to seriously reduce effectiveness, practitioners may decide to report them as feedback in order to stimulate efforts to improve communication between ranks. In other instances consultants may simply take note of divergent viewpoints, so as to avoid giving undue weight to one particular interpretation when formulating their own descriptions and analyses.

Interviews and questionnaire studies are often subject to bias because respondents seek to present themselves in a favorable light or withhold information, such as negative descriptions of supervisors, that they fear may ultimately be used against them. Practitioners can help overcome these concerns by gradually building relationships of trust with group members. Sometimes practitioners are able to develop such relationships with individuals who are highly knowledgeable about organizational affairs but somewhat detached from them, and are therefore willing to provide a great deal of valuable information.[3] Assistants to high-level managers, for example, may have a very comprehensive view of their organization and be more comfortable in describing it than the top managers themselves. When such well-placed individuals grow to trust consultants, they may provide useful information about sensitive subjects, such as the degree of influence of managers who are officially of equal authority or staff members' past reactions to risk-taking behavior (see Chapter 6 on ethical issues that arise in gathering and using such sensitive information).

Self-administered questionnaires. Self-administered questionnaires provide the least expensive way of eliciting the attitudes, beliefs, and opinions of large numbers of individuals. Aggregations of individual responses can also provide a substitute for behavioral measures of group-level phenomena. Although questionnaires typically use fixed-choice answers, a few open-ended questions can also be included to give respondents an opportunity to express themselves. Responses to such open-ended questions are often informative but hard to code. Questionnaires composed of items drawn from standardized organizational surveys (see below and Appendix B) can be prepared and administered rapidly because there is less need to develop and pretest the instrument. By including standard measures consultants may also be able to compare the responses obtained in the client organization with results from other organizations in which the same instrument was used.

Standardized instruments. One of the most useful standardized instruments is the Michigan Organizational Assessment Questionnaire—MOAQ (Cammann et al., 1983), which is part of a battery of instruments in the Michigan Quality of Work Program (Seashore et al., 1983). MOAQ is particularly well suited to the assessment of

3. Such individuals are called informants in academic research. I have avoided using the term here because of its negative connotations.

individual-level attitudes and beliefs. Practitioners may select one or more of its seven modules or choose appropriate questions from within modules. MOAQ's Module One covers the following important attitudes and psychological states:

—internal work motivation (satisfaction from doing the job well)
—intention to leave the organization or the job
—perceived ability to switch jobs
—satisfaction with the job and with the amount, fairness, and administration of pay
—the quality of the job (challenge, meaning, responsibility)
—identification with work and the organization
—perception that pay is based on performance
—self-report of the effort the respondent makes at work

The other modules in MOAQ expand the coverage of the factors measured in Module One and treat the following additional areas:

—respondent's personal background (including time in job and organization)
—adequacy of training and skills for present job
—job characteristics (hours, classification)
—importance of various types of rewards (pay, recognition, interest, freedom at work
—extent to which various rewards are felt to be tied to performance
—determinants of pay (tenure, job responsibility, experience, performance by individual, group, entire organization)
—role: clarity (know what is expected), overload (too much work), conflict (can't satisfy everyone)
—supervisor's behavior (participativeness, support, work facilitation, planning, control, goal setting, production orientation, fairness, race and sex bias)
—group characteristics (homogeneity of skills, backgrounds; cohesion— i.e., mutual attraction)
—group processes (goal clarity, involvement in decision making, opinions listened to, fragmentation—bickering, lack of mutual respect, etc.)

MOAQ could contribute significantly to a comprehensive diagnosis if additional behavioral data were obtained on individual or group outputs and if more data were gathered on group processes, structures, technology, and external relations. The Organization Assessment Instrument—OAI (Van de Ven & Ferry, 1980)—provides many scales in these areas, as well as items that overlap with MOAQ.

An additional feature of OAI is that it contains separate questionnaires for supervisors and group members, so that comparisons can
be made of their attitudes and reports. Other instruments within OAI
assess divisional (interdepartmental) and organization-level phenomena (see Chapter 4).

Here is a list of useful scales in OAI, organized in terms of the
categories used in Figure 2:

Group Composition, Structure, and Technology
—occupational specialization
—interchangeability of roles
—heterogeneity of members' skills
—concentration of authority in the hands of supervisors, group members,
  employee representatives, and outside authorities
—extent of automation
—standardization and specification of performance standards
—work flow: dependence of members on one another, on supervisor, on
  other groups
—interdependencies: segmented (members work independently), sequential, reciprocal, or team relations

Group Behavior, Processes, and Culture
—pressures for conformity to group norms
—communication (frequency and nature)
—conflict (within groups and with other units)
—conflict resolution methods
—strictness of control

Group Performance
—perceived unit performance (output quantity and quality, attainment of
  goals and targets, innovativeness efficiency, morale, reputation for
  excellence)

To obtain data on group-level phenomena from questionnaires
like MOAQ and OAI, the responses from members of a particular
work group or administrative unit are averaged to create group
scores. For these averages to be meaningful, the questionnaires must
specify clearly what work groups and which supervisors are referred
to, and the investigators must make sure that all members of a work
group refer to the same group in their responses. Otherwise the data
cannot be used in the diagnosis of specific groups or to provide feedback to group managers and members.

Advantages and drawbacks of standardized questionnaires. MOAQ
and OAI provide diagnostic tools that are extensively documented

and validated and reflect current research. Unlike earlier instruments (e.g., Blake & Mouton, 1964; Taylor & Bowers, 1972), which were based on models that advocated a single administrative style, these new assessment packages reflect the widely accepted view that there is no one best way to organize groups or organizations. Instead, the optimal combination of system traits is assumed to depend on many variables including the environment, tasks, technology, personnel, history, and size of the organization.

Despite their obvious appeal, standardized diagnostic instruments also have serious weaknesses and drawbacks. First, they may give practitioners a false sense of confidence that all the factors of relevance to a particular client organization have been covered adequately. Second, because standard questions are necessarily abstract, they may not be fully applicable to a particular organization or situation. For example, a typical questionnaire item asks respondents to indicate their degree of agreement with the statement, "My supervisor encourages subordinates to participate in making important decisions" (Cammann et al., 1983, p. 108). But the responses to this general statement may mask the fact that the supervisor encourages participation in decisions in one area, such as work scheduling, while making decisions alone in other areas, such as budgeting. To obtain data on such situational variations, investigators must first determine the situations across which there may be broad variations and then write specific questions about these situations (e.g., Moch et al., 1983a, pp. 199–200).

Third, as in any questionnaire, even apparently simple questions may contain concepts or phrases that may be understood in different ways. For instance, when reacting to the statement, "I get to do a number of different things on my job" (Cammann et al., 1983, p. 94), one person may see diversity in physical actions (e.g., snipping versus scraping) or minor changes in the tools needed for the job, whereas another would consider all of those operations as "doing the same thing." Fourth, questionnaires are especially vulnerable to biases stemming from the respondent's desire to give socially acceptable answers or avoid sensitive issues. There may also be tendencies to give consistent responses (Salancik & Pfeffer, 1977). Some instruments include questions designed to detect or minimize biases, whereas others (e.g., Taylor & Bowers, 1972) may heighten bias by phrasing all questions in a single direction.

Observations. Observation can help consultants get a first-hand feel for the kinds of behavior and processes that occur within an organization and develop interpretations of situations that depend less on members attitudes and viewpoints than do data from questionnaires and interviews. People are often not very good observers of the actions occurring within their groups and often cannot describe group norms, beliefs, and informal behavior patterns or are reluctant to do so. Because observation is time consuming and requires keen observational skills, it is often reserved for the analysis of top management groups, whose decisions and solutions to problems are critical to the organization as a whole.

Observational techniques. Observations may be structured in terms of a general accounting scheme, such as the *Questions about Group Meetings*, below (see also Perkins et al., 1981) or in terms of predefined categories for coding observed behavior (see Weick, 1985, for examples). Experienced practitioners may also conduct unstructured observations so as to remain open to unanticipated phenomena.

Unless a highly structured coding scheme is used, observers record the behavior of the participants. Here are some examples:

"Chairperson shouts for order."
"Workers consult each other over how to get the machine going again."
"Nurses are quiet, do not participate in the discussion of the case."

Notations on observed behavior like these provide the data on which subsequent inferences about group functioning are based. For example, repeated observations of workers helping each other handle snags in operations may lead consultants to conclude that relationships between workers are cooperative and facilitate independence from supervisors and technicians. Including such concrete descriptions of behavior will also make feedback more useful to group members. If observations are guided by a list of topics, observers can summarize their findings for each topic and then add illustrative descriptions from the original notes.

Before beginning their observations of a particular setting, investigators often try to learn as much as possible through interviews or informal conversations about the backgrounds of the people to be observed, their roles, the nature of the task facing the group, and the ways that this task or similar ones have been handled in the past. If note taking during the observations will disturb group members, then observers should record their notes as soon as possible after the conclusion of the observation. With practice it is possible to develop the ability to recall entire conversations or discussions and to record them after completing the observation. Things that the observer did not understand can be clarified through repeated observations or through discussions with participants. Additional observations of the group under differing circumstances and repeated observations of similar events will help the observer distinguish between recurring and one-time phenomena. Once a clear picture has emerged, the results can be compared to those obtained from other data sources and can be prepared for analysis and feedback.

A guide to diagnosing meeting behavior. To illustrate observational techniques, let us consider how practitioners might observe group meetings. Meetings make an ideal focus for observations. Managers and salaried professionals spend much of their time in meetings, and meeting outcomes form an important part of managerial outputs. Moreover, participants often find meetings to be frustrating and unproductive. Hence, they may be interested in having consultants diagnose meeting behavior and helping them improve group effectiveness.

Researchers and consultants with experience in sensitivity training and organization development have created a variety of schemes for observing and diagnosing group functioning that can be applied to the observation of meetings (e.g., Benne & Sheats, 1948; Schein, 1969). These observational frames usually reflect the assumption mentioned above that groups work better when there is an open sharing of information and feelings, deemphasis on status and power differences and participatory decision making. As research (Alderfer, 1977; Porras & Berg, 1978; Strauss, 1976) has shown that no single set of group features always contributes to group effectiveness, the diagnostic questions below do not presuppose a single form of optimal group functioning. Instead, they ask about important group processes while allowing practitioners to draw their own conclusions about the importance and impact of each factor. Because the questions are only a guide to observations, they do not provide instructions about what particular behaviors to note or how to make inferences from them. Thus, to answer each of these diagnostic questions, observers will have to consult their notes on the *behavior observed* during the meeting (e.g., shouting between two members), decide how much they can *generalize* from these observations (e.g., members often shout at one another), and make appropriate *inferences* from the observations (e.g., shouting shows that members take differences of opinion personally). Users are encouraged to select among the questions, to modify them, and to apply them so as to fit the particular features of the group being observed and incorporate relevant effectiveness criteria. Besides guiding observations, these questions can provide a framework for feedback and could also be used by groups wishing to engage in self-diagnosis.

*Questions about Group Meetings—For Observation
or Self-Diagnosis*

(1) *Goals, targets, and procedures*—Are the goals of the meeting or the problems to be dealt with stated in advance? Are clear guidelines given for the time and resources to be devoted toward reaching these ends? Do the participants understand and accept the goals and purposes of the meeting and of the group, or do people seem to have different, hidden agendas for the meeting?

(2) *Participation*—Do participants other than the leader share in developing the goals and guidelines for the meeting? Do most people participate, or do a few talk most of the time? How much airing of divergent opinions occurs? Do participants have the time and ability to examine the information they are given? Are they prepared for the discussion?

(3) *The flow of information and ideas*—Are there opportunities for the clarification and development of the ideas and proposals presented? Are ideas and proposals adequately summarized so that participants can keep track of their progress? How much does the chairperson guide and control the discussion? Does the group move easily from one issue to another, or must these shifts be forced on them by the leader or by a few participants?

(4) *Problem solving*—Do the participants define clearly the problems facing them and search for alternative solutions before deciding? Are long-term consequences of actions considered as well as short-term ones? Is more than one alternative considered, and are dissenting opinions considered by others, or is there a tendency for "groupthink"—where everyone backs one solution without seriously discussing others? Do participants draw on past experiences and learn from them? Do they consider new ideas and solutions to problems, as well as familiar, time-tested ones?

(5) *Decision making*—What kinds of procedures are used to decide on the various proposals raised—ignoring the proposal, acceptance or rejection by top authorities, decision by a minority of powerful participants, voting, consensus? Do participants seem to accept these methods? Do these methods seem to produce the best decisions? Do important issues go undecided?

(6) *Conflict*—What important conflicts arise during the meeting? How are they handled—by someone forcing a solution, by one party back-

ing down, by bargaining, or by collaboration in finding a mutually satisfying solution? What are the impacts of these conflict-resolution methods (e.g., members seem angry, alienated, anxious to work together)? Do conflicts stimulate thinking and problem solving or disrupt the meeting?

(7) *Interpersonal relations and feelings*—How cohesive is the group? Do differences among members interfere with their working together? Are there opportunities for enhancing group solidarity? What kinds of verbal and nonverbal behavior provide cues to participants' feelings (e.g., exclamations, tone of voice, posture)? Do members seem to trust one another? Do they listen to one another or interrupt and ignore others? Do they discuss differences of opinion in terms of common standards and values, or do they treat them as personal conflicts? Do they find the meetings satisfying or frustrating?

(8) *Outcomes*—What are the major outcomes of the meeting—solutions, decisions, proposals, ideas, and so on? Are their implications for action spelled out clearly—including responsibilities for executing them, the time allotted for doing so, and the forms of follow-up and evaluation? How satisfied with the outcomes of the meeting are its participants, leaders, and others who are affected by the group's work? How well do the outcomes meet other relevant effectiveness criteria (e.g., innovativeness, adaptiveness)?

To decide how important each of the listed items is to group functioning and to decide whether a particular feature, such as participation in decision making, is critical to group effectiveness, practitioners will have to define clearly what effectiveness criteria they want to apply and will need to trace the impacts of the feature on effectiveness. Consider, for example, the question of whether participants in the meeting shared in developing goals and guidelines for action. If consultants regard the satisfactions and feelings of group members as important indicators of effectiveness, then participation in goal setting may be seen as a condition that is likely to facilitate effectiveness. But the impact of this condition can depend on the nature and context of the group. Group members who are highly educated and accustomed to having their professional opinions taken seriously by others are likely to resent having goals and procedures imposed upon them. In contrast, in organizations with more authoritarian traditions, such as military organizations, members accept having goals and procedures set for them, and their satisfactions may depend more on their group's outputs than on their participation in goal setting.

Analysis

The same logical and statistical procedures that are used in nonapplied research can be used to analyze diagnostic data (e.g., Lofland, 1971; Schatzman & Strauss, 1973; Selltiz et al., 1981). Once summarized, nonstatistical data can be analyzed with the help of diagrams like Figure 2. The main findings about each of the categories shown there could be recorded on an enlarged version of the figure. The arrows between the boxes in the figure could then be labeled to describe important system interactions. If, for example, an assembly-line technology seemed to be producing boredom and alienation among workers, this relationship could be shown on the figure. Beneath the figure supporting evidence of the relationship could be recorded—such as the observation that workers who were transferred to other less routine operations at equal pay showed higher motivation and less boredom.

If the study included standard, quantifiable measures on which data exists for other organizations, comparisons can be made between the findings for the client organization and these baseline data. More frequently, statistical or qualitative comparisons can be made between all similar units (e.g., work teams) within the organization on all of the effectiveness measures and on variables that are assumed to add to effectiveness. Then, groups that are unusually high or low on the measures can be isolated for further study, or the data can be prepared for feedback to group members. Alternatively, if previous investigations suggested that certain units are particularly outstanding or problematic in some important feature, such as innovativeness, consultants may concentrate on examining the characteristics of these units.

Before undertaking extended multivariate analyses of questionnaire data, practitioners should decide how heavily their diagnosis will rely on these analyses. Alternatively, they could use other methods to gather additional information or provide members of the client group with the major single or bivariate distributions and encourage them to try to account for the findings in terms of their own understandings of the organization. Whatever approach is chosen, the data should be presented in a form that is appealing and easy to understand. Reports and trade literature that are circulating within a client organization will usually provide indications of appropriate formats for presenting data.

Feedback

Procedures. There are wide variations in the possible procedures
for providing feedback from diagnostic studies (see Nadler, 1977).
Sometimes practitioners only give feedback to the client or clients
who called for the study. More frequently, where feedback is viewed
as a means of encouraging group problem solving, consultants
present their results to all the participants in the study or to everyone
who is affected by its findings. The supervisors and members of an
organizational unit can be given relevant feedback at the same time
or separately. The major danger in providing feedback simultaneously to supervisors and subordinates is that supervisors often experience conflicts between being made a target of criticism and being
expected to lead the discussion about the planning of appropriate
action. An alternative design involves providing feedback to task
forces or other temporary groups that cut across departmental and
hierarchical lines. These groups are assigned responsibility for planning the organization's response to the findings.

Sometimes the feedback is restricted to a single oral or written
presentation of findings and recommendations. In contrast, organization-development consultants usually try to collaborate with members
of the client organization in interpreting the findings and deciding
how to deal with them (see Burke, 1982, p. 162, and Chapter 1,
"Participation in Diagnosisa ..."). First, the consultant presents a
summary of the data and a preliminary analysis. A discussion
usually follows in which the findings are clarified. Finally, the practitioner and the group members discuss the interpretation of the data
and their implications for action.

Feedback characteristics. Whatever form feedback takes, people are
more likely to accept and act upon it when the feedback has the
following features (Block, 1981; Huse & Cummings, 1985, pp. 78-79;
see also Chapter 6):

(1) Relevant and understandable to members
(2) Descriptive, rather than evaluative
(3) Clear and specific—referring to concrete behavior and situations,
     illustrating generalizations, and providing comparisons between
     groups
(4) Given shortly after data gathering
(5) Believable—providing information about the validity of the data
(6) Sensitive to members' feelings and motivations—rather than provok-
     ing anger, defensiveness, or feelings of helplessness

(7) Limited, rather than overwhelming
(8) Practical and feasible—pointing to issues that members can do something about
(9) Open-ended—leaving room for members to make their own interpretations and decide how to act

Practitioners can improve their feedback by adopting procedures that correspond more closely to these standards, even if it is impossible to conform to them in full.

EXERCISES

1. Using Questionnaires to Diagnose Group Processes

Choose two work groups or units on which background information is available. These groups should perform similar tasks and have similar types of employees. Try to locate one group reputed to have positive features (e.g., high quality of work life or positive supervisor-subordinate relations), and another that seems to be weak in the same areas. Develop a questionnaire on key aspects of group process with around 10 questions drawn from one or more of the standardized questionnaires discussed in this chapter and in Appendix B. Distribute the questionnaire to members of both groups after you have explained that the data will only be used for an exercise and will not be distributed to anyone outside the groups. Prepare a summary of the average responses to each question for the groups and compare your results to the previous information you had on the groups. If the results differ from what you expected, try to account for these differences. Explain how you would give feedback to the supervisors and members of both groups in order to facilitate constructive discussion and problem solving. If requested, prepare a separate summary of the findings for each new group.

2. Observing Meetings

Use the *Questions about Group Meetings* as a guide to observing at least two meetings of the same group. Write a report covering the following topics:

(1) Background on the groups and the meetings (type of meetings, purpose, circumstances—e.g., routine weekly meeting, emergency session, etc.—participants, organizational context, etc.)
(2) Summary of observations of group processes (organized in terms of the topics listed in the *Questions about Group Meetings* or a consolidated set of topics)
(3) Criteria for evaluating group effectiveness
(4) Sources of effectiveness and ineffectiveness
(5) Possible ways of improving effectiveness
(6) Ways to provide feedback to participants

4

Examining System Fits and Power Relations within Divisions and Organizations

The open system model is used as a guide to assessing the fits between such elements as structure, environment, technology, and goals. Emphasis is placed on aspects of the organization design that managers can influence. Fits between actual behavior and official objectives and practices are also discussed. The final part of the chapter treats ways to assess the distribution and uses of power—one of the most critical aspects of actual behavior.

As noted in the preceding chapter, conditions at the divisional and organizational levels can contribute to group and individual problems such as low levels of satisfaction, poor task performance, high turnover, and tense interpersonal relations. When most groups within a division or an entire organization suffer from such problems, their sources are likely to lie in broader, higher-level conditions, rather than being caused mainly by group-level factors, such as the behavior of particular supervisors or the structure of particular work groups. In addition, divisional or organizationwide forces may contribute to other kinds of problems involving several departments or groups, including,

—conflicts between units
—tasks being neglected or "falling between the cracks"
—lack of innovation
—failure to cope with changing market or technical conditions
—communication delays and failures
—inability to carry out complex projects

This chapter shows how to diagnose the causes of such divisional and organizational problems by examining the fits between system elements or between their subcomponents. The terms *fit, congruence,* or *alignment* refer to the extent to which the behavioral or organizational requirements and the constraints in one part of a system are compatible with those in other parts (Beer, 1980; Kotter, 1978; Nadler & Tushman, 1980a, 1980b).[1]

DIAGNOSING SYSTEM FITS

Introduction

Here is a case (Beckhard, 1975, p. 52) that illustrates the potential impacts of fits between system elements at the division level:

> The head of a major corporate division was frustrated by the lack of motivation of his subordinates to work with him on planning for the future of the business as a whole and their lack of attention to developing the managerial potential of their own subordinates. Repeated exhortations about these matters produced few results, although the division managers agreed that change was desirable. The barrier to change was that these managers were held directly accountable for short-term profits in their division. There were no meaningful rewards for engaging in planning or management development and no punishments for not doing so, but had the managers failed to show a profit, they would have been fired on the spot.

This case shows the impact of poor fit between the decision's objectives (purposes) and its reward mechanisms—a component of its structure. The division's objectives included planning and management development, but its reward and control procedures discouraged managers from contributing to their subordinates and instead led them to strive exclusively for more tangible, short-term results.

Figure 3 provides a schematic summary of the steps required to diagnose fits. The first step in the figure, the choice of fits, is treated in the section that follows immediately. The second and third steps are addressed in the sections "Ways to Assess Fit," "Diagnosing Organization Design," and "Actual Practices." The fourth step is discussed in the section "Assessing the Impacts of Fits."

1. It is also possible to examine fits between different system levels, for example, individual-group, individual-organization, group-organization fits (see Nadler & Tushman, 1980a).

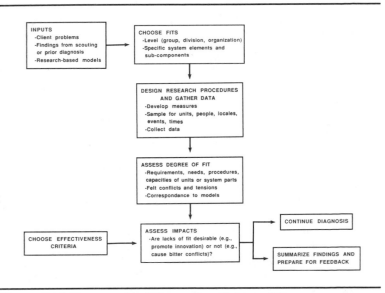

Figure 3: A Process for Diagnosing System Fits

The Choice of Fits

A checklist of important fits. One way to choose fits for diagnosis is to start with a checklist, like the one shown in Table 5 of fits that research and consulting practice have shown to be especially important. A comprehensive diagnostic study could examine each of these fits in at least a preliminary fashion. Because the divisions of large, complex organizations will differ from one another in all or most of the system elements (e.g., environment, technology, structure), it is best to begin by examining fits within divisions. If necessary, fits within the total organization can be considered subsequently.

Starting with client problems. A more focused and practical approach is to examine those fits that are more directly related to the problems that clients present or that showed up during scouting. For example, the practitioner who encounters complaints about tasks being neglected or handled poorly can deal with these complaints and clarify the links between structure, decision making, and communication through *responsibility charting*, a procedure that has been used in many large corporations (Galbraith, 1977, p. 171). First, during interviews or workshops group members are asked to list key

TABLE 5
Questions about Fits

Focal Area	Does focal area fit with . . .
Human Resources	*Structure, Technology, Processes:*
	Do employees' skills and training fit their job requirements? (Chapter 3)*
	Are the best people attracted and retained by the rewards and advancement opportunities offered? (Chapter 3)
	Are professionals and others seeking autonomy and challenge assigned to less structured and less closely controlled jobs? (Chapters 3 & 4; Lorsch & Morse, 1974)
Purposes	*Resources:*
	Can the organization's strategies and programs be supported by available resources? (Chapters 2 & 5; Andrews, 1971; Nadler & Tushman, 1980a)
	Environment:
	Do the division's strategies, tactics, and objectives help it gain and maintain a favorable position in its environment? (Chapter 5; Andrews, 1971; Porter, 1980)
	Behavior, Processes, Culture:
	Does management express its purposes in ways that create a sense of mission and identity among members? (Pfeffer, 1981a)
	Are efforts to change the division compatible with current norms, behavior, and assumptions? (Chapter 2; Argyris & Schon, 1978; Davis, 1984)
	Technology, Behavior, Processes:
	Do managerial plans and objectives contribute to work, or are they too inflexible to handle unforeseen developments? (McCaskey, 1979; Newman & Warren, 1977; Quinn, 1980)

Technology   *Structure:*

Are those people who must work together closely
grouped in units or otherwise linked structurally?
(Chapter 4; Beer, 1980, pp. 159–168; Khandwalla,
1977)

Are the procedures for coordinating work and
information flows appropriate to the tasks and
the technology? Are tasks that are poorly understood or require creativity and innovation
handled by organic structures? (Chapter 4;
Galbraith, 1977; Tushman & Nadler, 1978)

Structure, Behavior:

Are there tasks and functions that no one is
doing adequately and others on which people or
units overlap needlessly? (Chapter 4)

Structure   *Behavior, Processes, Culture:*

Do members regard official rules and procedures
as fair and sensible? (Chapter 3)

Do reward and control mechanisms encourage
behavior and group norms that are compatible
with managerial objectives? (Chapter 4; Lawler &
Rhode, 1976)

Technology, Environment:

Are the structures of the divisions (or their subunits) differentiated enough to allow them to
handle the special problems created by their particular environments, technologies, and tasks?
Are the coordinating mechanisms adequate for
the level of differentiation? (Chapter 4;
Galbraith, 1977; Lawrence & Lorsch, 1969)

Technology, Processes:

Does the physical and geographic layout of the
division contribute to the flow of work and information? (Steele, 1973)

Official Purposes,   *Actual Behavior, Processes, Culture:*
Structures,
Processes   Are managerial objectives and procedures
supported by actual norms and behavior?
(Chapter 4; Nadler & Tushman, 1980a)

Actual Behavior, Processes:

Are group actions and decisions blocked by
bitter conflicts or power struggles? (Chapter 4)

Does undesirable competition between units
result from departmental specialization or from
rewards and controls encouraging competition?
(Chapter 4; Pondy, 1967; Walton & Dutton, 1969)

Do people and units have enough power and
resources to accomplish their tasks adequately?
(Chapter 4; Kanter, 1979)

---

*References are to chapters of this book and to other sources in which the question is explored more fully.

tasks or decision areas. In a project group these might include
budgeting, scheduling, allocating personnel, and changing design
specifications of the product. Second, each member is asked to list
the positions that might be involved in these areas (e.g., project director, general manager, laboratory manager) and to indicate who is
assigned *responsibilty* for performing tasks and who else is supposed
to *approve* the tasks performed, *be consulted*, and *be informed* about it.
The data usually reveal ambiguities relating to one or more task
areas. These data can be used as feedback to stimulate efforts to
redefine responsibilities and clarify relationships, and they can lead
clients and consultants to examine fundamental organizational
features, such as the degree of delegation of authority, communication patterns, and the division of labor. For example, discussion of
approval procedures for work scheduling may reveal that many
minor changes are needed and that scheduling would operate more
smoothly if middle-level managers received the authority to make
such minor changes and to inform the project head afterwards. By
starting with client concerns and then branching out in this fashion,
consultants may find ways of dealing with pressing problems while
also uncovering conditions that can have a wider impact on organizational effectiveness.

Fits involving design tools. Consultants to management often concentrate their diagnoses on fits involving *design tools*, organizational
arrangements like job responsibilities that can most readily be
redesigned by their clients (Beer, 1980). As the case of the corporate
division cited above suggests, the procedures used in rewarding,
monitoring, and evaluating performance are among the most power-

ful design tools. In that case the division head was able to build incentives for planning and management development into the reward system by recalculating bonus pay to reflect contributions in these areas.

Here are some other design tools to consider (Beer, 1980, p. 27; Mintzberg, 1979):

—the structural grouping of positions and units
—job designs
—personnel policies (i.e., recruitment, selection, training, advancement, compensation, labor relations)
—management-information systems
—mechanisms for coordinating units or positions
—performance-control procedures
—accounting and budgeting systems
—geographic location and physical layout

Design tools can structure the options available to members and create pressures to act in a particular fashion. Such administrative measures may ultimately shape the organizational culture by establishing official rules of the game according to which members must play if they wish to remain and advance in the organization. These impacts show up, for example, in the effects of task definitions, rewards, and control procedures on interdepartmental conflict (Pondy, 1967; Walton & Dutton, 1969). When departments are evaluated solely on the basis of how well they have achieved their objectives, their members lack incentives for interdepartmental cooperation. Instead, they are encouraged to compete with other departments for scarce resources and do everything in their power to "look good" at evaluation time. Competition and conflict between groups will be further heightened by rewards that are tied to outperforming other departments. In contrast, interdepartmental cooperation can be enhanced by evaluating departments on their contributions to attaining divisional or organizationwide objectives that require cooperation.

The greater the authority and autonomy of clients, the more readily they can make changes in these design factors. Collective bargaining agreements, government regulations, and internal opposition may severely restrict the options available to both public and private sector managers.

Ways to Assess Fits

One way to assess fits is to examine the compatibility of the requirements, needs, or procedures of different units or system parts. The fits between units are weak if the work of one unit, such as the medical staff of a hospital outpatient clinic, is disrupted because of inadequate inputs from another unit, such as the x-ray department. Incompatibility between units and system parts often appears in divergent or conflicting messages about the kinds of behavior required. In a newspaper bureau, for example, the official job responsibilities of reporters included suggesting topics for stories, but the reporters learned from their experiences in staff meetings that it did not pay to challenge the editor's leadership in this area.

A second way to assess fit is to investigate whether participants *feel* subject to conflicting expectations or pressures and to check whether these conflicts are the result of lacks of fit. In the case of the corporate division described above, for example, a sales manager might have complained during an interview, "My boss wants me to work on management development, but if I do, I'll be in hot water when he goes over my quarterly sales results!" The practitioner would then check whether other managers made similar comments and whether rewards were indeed closely tied to quarterly performance, while ignoring management development activities.

A third possibility is to see whether system elements or components fit together in ways that research-based models suggest they should (e.g., Miles & Snow, 1978; Mintzberg, 1979; Nightingale & Tolouse, 1977). The following section describes models of organization design that can help practitioners assess the fits between the structures of organizations and divisions and other system elements. Other useful models for diagnosing fits are referred to in the references to Table 5.

Diagnosing Organization Design

Fits between work-flow and coordination mechanisms. One useful model specifies the types of coordination procedures required by the technology (Galbraith, 1977; Thompson, 1967; Tichy, 1983; Tushman & Nadler, 1978). According to this model, work technologies create three different kinds of *interdependencies* in the work flow:

Pooled interdependencies—where units can work independently of each other (e.g., crews in a home construction firm)

Sequential interdependencies—where work must flow from one unit to another in a clearly defined sequence (e.g., assembly line)

Reciprocal interdependencies—where units must adjust to each other (e.g., sales and design groups tailor product or service to customer needs)

When the technology creates pooled interdependencies, operations can be coordinated by rules, standard operating procedures (e.g., "Discard parts that exceed standard by .003mm"), and supervision from above. When work must flow sequentially, rules and procedures must be supplemented by more detailed planning of the relationships between units, closer monitoring of unit outputs, and more supervision from above. But these familiar coordination mechanisms do not fit the requirements of technologies that create reciprocal interdependencies between units. Coordination mechanisms that build in *lateral relations* between units best fit these needs for two-way communication and mutual adjustment. These mechanisms include teams, committees, and flexible, integrative roles such as product managers (see "Differentiation and integration," below).

To examine fits between work flow interdependencies and coordination mechanisms, practitioners can observe operations or interview members about work flows between units. Interunit coordination is problematic if members view these coordination procedures as clumsy or inadequate, or if interunit contacts are characterized by frequent interruptions, misunderstandings, surprises, and high levels of conflict. In such cases members may not be using current coordinating mechanisms adequately, or these mechanisms may be inappropriate to the types of interdependencies.

Organic versus mechanistic systems. Sometimes findings from diagnoses at lower levels or client requests (e.g., Chapter 1, "Introduction," Case 1) can lead consultants to assess the design of an entire organization or that of a complex, highly autonomous division. Table 6 summarizes a useful model for assessing fits between the administrative system (structure, processes, and culture) of a division or organization and its environment, technology, and personnel (Burns & Stalker, 1961; Lawrence & Lorsch, 1969; Tichy, 1983; Tushman & Nadler, 1978). This model can also be applied to smaller units like departments.

TABLE 6
Conditions Affecting the Fit of
Mechanistic and Organic Systems

Description*	Mechanistic	Organic
Roles, Responsibilities	Specialized, clearly defined.	Diffuse, flexible, change through use.
Coordination and Control	Supervision, rules, standard procedures, detailed plans; frequent evaluation based on meeting objectives, standards.	Consultation among all having related tasks; flexible plans, diffuse, changing goals; evaluation of results over longer time frame.
Communication	Top-down emphasis: top management has key outside contacts.	Multidirectional: multilevel contacts with outsiders.
Supervision and Leadership	Nonparticipative, one-on-one: loyalty to superiors stressed: position and experience grant authority.	Participative, team styles: emphasis on task, team, organization; expertise & knowledge grant authority.
Sources of Knowledge	Local, internal.	External, cosmopolitan: professional orientation.

Fit best when		
Technology is . . .	Routine (well understood, standardized.	Nonroutine (not well understood; or designed for each problem).
Task environment is . . .	Predictable (simple, changing predictably).	Unpredictable (complex, changing rapidly).
Personnel expect . . .	High level of structure and routine; control from above.	High levels of role flexibility, challenging work.

Effectiveness criteria stress . . .	Efficiency; standard, predictable operations and outputs; ease of control from top.	Creativity, innovativeness, adaptiveness, quality of work life, development of human resources.

*See Burns & Stalker (1961), Tichy (1983, p. 276)

Organic systems provide greater information-processing capacity, encourage creativity and innovativeness, and facilitate rapid, flexible responses to change. In addition, they provide more interesting and challenging work environments than *mechanistic systems*. On the other hand, they are more costly and harder to administer. Hence, when conditions are predictable, the rules, standard operating procedures, and top-down supervision in mechanistic systems often yield more efficient and productive results than do organic arrangements. From this standpoint mechanistic arrangements are well suited to the provision of routine services in government (e.g., postal service) and the private sector (e.g., homeowners' insurance), as well as to many routine manufacturing operations (e.g., manufacturing toys). In contrast, the organic administrative style can help divisions or entire firms adapt to uncertainties stemming from poorly understood and changing technological conditions (e.g., in developing microelectronic products, cancer research), and from unpredictable environmental conditions—such as markets subject to sudden changes of taste and unstable financial conditions.

The administrative system also needs to fit the prevailing technology. If the technical tasks are well understood and the available technology makes it possible to break the work down into routine operations (e.g., assembly-line manufacturing, processing of applicants for food stamps), then mechanistic forms of coordination and control can effectively guide production or treatment processes and will usually be less costly (Perrow, 1970). In contrast, when technical tasks are poorly understood or resist standardization (e.g., design of new product. development of advertising campaign), organic arrangements are needed to allow for innovativeness, creativity, and flexibility.

Finally, administrative patterns need to fit the background and expectations of the work force (Lorsch & Morse, 1974). Organic systems will better fit the work style of employees who have been professionally trained to regulate their own work and to adjust to the needs and expectations of peers. Organic systems will also provide higher quality of working life for nonprofessional employees who seek greater autonomy and more challenging work (see Chapter 3). Unfortunately, when the work can be done using routine procedures, the introduction of more organic forms of administration may require expensive reorganizations and technological changes and may not raise outputs or cut operating costs.

To use the mechanistic-organic systems model in diagnosis, practitioners need to assess how organic or mechanistic a division's current administrative system is and how well the current system fits the conditions and effectiveness criteria listed in Table 6. Employee expectations can be measured directly (see Chapter 3 and Van de Ven & Ferry, 1980, p. 392). Chapter 5 provides details on assessing environmental conditions.

Standardized measures can also be used to assess many of the administrative features summarized in Table 6. Separate indices can be created for each of the dimensions shown in the upper half of the table, or a single combined index can be constructed. One advantage of examining each dimension separately is that low levels of fit may be found between these administrative dimensions. For example, a division head may try to encounter managers to work together on innovative projects but may inadvertently block team work by retaining a one-on-one style of supervision.

Taken as a whole, systems may be considered too mechanistic if they face very unpredictable environments and nonroutine tasks. In particular, a division may need a more organic system if it is unable to cope with the following three types of challenges:

(1) Adapt to change and respond rapidly and decisively to threats and opportunities
(2) Handle nonroutine tasks in innovative and creative ways
(3) Meet employee expectations for creative, challenging work

On the other hand, unless staff development or quality of working life is very important, divisions that use organic arrangements to handle predictable external conditions and routine tasks are probably failing to take advantage of efficiencies that could be obtained by introducing more mechanistic procedures. If a preliminary application of the model suggests that change is needed in either direction, practitioners can focus more closely on those design tools that clients can most readily change.

Divisionalization. A key question in the diagnosis of the structure of total organizations and divisions concerns the ways that units are grouped together. When consultants examine an organization's current form of divisionalization, they should investigate whether people and units that must work together intensively are located in the same administrative units or in close contact with one another. In addition they should consider whether the structure keeps costs to a minimum by avoiding unnecessary duplication of positions and underuse of resources, and whether it provides sufficient adaptiveness to variations in markets and other environmental conditions (e.g., degree of governmental regulation of products or production processes). As a rule, organizations that are divisionalized along *functional* lines (e.g., marketing, engineering, production) are less able to respond to divergencies in markets and other environmental conditions than those divisionalized in terms of *products and services* (e.g., life, home, and commercial insurance divisions), or in terms of *markets or geographical areas* (Mintzberg, 1979). However, there are many variations within types and many opportunities for combining them.

Differentiation and integration. The more the tasks, technology, and environments of divisions or other major subunits vary from one another, the more the divisional structures will have to be *differentiated* (Lawrence & Lorsch, 1969). For example, in a clothing firm with a division catering to the fashion trade (unpredictable environment) and one supplying uniforms to hospitals and other institutions (more stable environment), the fashion division would need to be more organic than the one supplying uniforms. The need for differentiation also stems from many other types of divergences in tasks, environments, and work force, such as legal conditions, levels of training of the work force, and the size of production runs, that are not summarized in the mechanistic-organic model. To assess whether an organization is sufficiently differentiated, practitioners need to decide whether each division is allowed to adapt sufficiently to its own objectives, technology, environment, and personnel. There is too much differentiation if there are unjustifiable divergences in administrative practices or other system features.

Once organizations become differentiated internally, they face serious problems of *integration* (coordination) across divisions (Lawrence & Lorsch, 1969). If an organization is highly differentiated, the mechanistic forms of coordination and control listed in Table 6 are not likely to provide sufficient levels of integration. To accommodate great divergence between divisions, top management can grant them greater autonomy and monitor divisional *results* (as opposed to monitoring operations), or management can create more *lateral linkages* between units and divisions that must work together (Galbraith, 1977; Mintzberg, 1979; Tichy, 1983). The list that follows ranks popular forms of lateral integration from the least to most complex:

(1) Direct contact between units
(2) Integrator and liason roles (e.g., coordinator of hospital geriatric services)
(3) Task forces and committees that temporarily unite members of several units
(4) Projects groups and teams that make these links more permanent
(5) Matrix structures with dual (functional and project) authority lines

In a matrix structure people retain their ties to a functional specialization, like computer services or sales, while serving in semipermanent product or market groups (e.g., "Talking Typewriter Project"). Matrix structures and other complex lateral integrating mechanisms can help organizations coordinate highly differentiated operations and cope with unpredictable environments and non-routine technologies. On the other hand, they are costly and hard to administer (Davis & Lawrence, 1977). Consultants should therefore weigh carefully the possibilities for using simpler lateral coordination mechanisms or increasing divisional autonomy before considering elaborate, risky reorganizations along matrix lines.

Actual Practices Versus Official Mandates

As in other forms of diagnosis, to examine many of the system fits listed in Table 5 practitioners need to distinguish between actual observable patterns of behavior and official descriptions of organizational life.[2] Official descriptions can provide useful insights into management's image of the organization's desired state, but they cannot serve as data on organizational behavior and practice.

2. The terms "actual" behavior and behavior "in practice" are preferable to the popular term "informal behavior." Formalization refers to the specification or programming of behavior and procedures in advance, often in writing (Hall, 1982, pp. 95–113). Thus, directives, goals, and structures can be official and authoritative without being formalized.

Examining actual practices. As noted in previous chapters, actual practices can diverge greatly from official descriptions of these practices and from official purposes and procedures. Managers, for example, may report that they frequently consult with their subordinates before reaching important decisions, but the subordinates' own reports and other sources of data on decision making may not confirm this idealized picture. What happens, for instance, when subordinates have bad news for their supervisors or hold different opinions from them (Argyris & Schon, 1978)? Actual features of other key processes (see Chapters 2 & 3)—including controlling and rewarding, supervision, and conflict management—should also be carefully examined.

Here is a listing of actual practices that practitioners may find diverge substantially from officially mandated ones:

(1) Operative goals and priorities as shown by decisions about resource allocation (e.g., budgeting, staffing)

(2) Informal structures (e.g., cliques, working ties that cut across departmental lines, end runs around immediate superiors to higher authorities; grapevines that bypass official communication channels)

(3) Role definitions and group functions in practice (e.g., actual division of labor, definitions of tasks, responsibilities, etc.)

(4) Informal leaders, influence patterns, and power relations (see below)

(5) Actual work procedures (e.g., cutting corners on safety, quality checks, reporting, record keeping; improvising solutions and procedures)

(6) Everyday beliefs (culture)—about payoffs (or penalties) for hard work and initiative; the tasks and conditions facing the organizations (e.g., "We're about to get bought out. Quit while you can!"); the kinds of information that can be taken seriously (e.g., "The forecasts from sales are always too optimistic.")

Collecting data on actual practices. Because actual organizational practices often run counter to official mandates, it is usually necessary to gather data on them through direct observations, intensive interviewing, or the analysis of organizational records. If respondents are especially cooperative and candid, data on informal social and working relationships can be obtained from sociometric questionnaires, in which respondents name people or positions with whom they work closely or have frequent contact (Moch et al., 1983b; Tichy et al., 1980). The patterns of one-way and mutual choice between respondents can then be analyzed to provide maps of relationships. Alternatively, questions about group leadership and work relations can be incorporated into open interviews.

Open or semistructured interviews should obtain explicit descriptions of how the respondents act in a range of work situations, rather than generalizations or expressions of attitudes, because explicit behavioral reports are somewhat less subject to bias than generalizations or attitudes. For instance, to obtain data about the actual division of labor within a project group, practitioners could ask several members to describe what each member of the group did during the design phase of a project and then draw the appropriate conclusion after examining all of these data. This procedure is more likely to yield valid results than asking members to generalize about whether "responsibilities are clear" in the group or asking attitudinal questions (e.g., "Are task assignments flexible enough to allow for unforeseen circumstances?").

Useful techniques for studying organizational cultures and practices include asking individual respondents or groups of members to describe the history of the organization or unit (Leach, 1979) or requesting accounts of organizational successes and failures (Argyris & Schon, 1978, pp. 32–48). In analyzing such accounts, close attention should be paid to assumptions and behavior that members take for granted (see Chapter 6, "Helping clients develop the capacity for self-examination").

Another fruitful strategy is to gather data from organizational records and from interviews concerning the entire process by which an idea, service, or product moves through the organization. In a study of hospital coordination mechanisms, for example, practitioners might trace the entire course of treatment of representative hospital patients, from reception to release. In a study of decision making and relationships in a product design unit they might follow a new product from its earliest design stages until it goes into routine production.

An advantage of direct observations and the analysis of existing data is that much information may be obtained *unobtrusively* (Webb et al., 1966), without interfering with people's behavior or influencing it. For example, by observing attendance at meetings or by checking records, practitioners may discover that a project that is officially assigned high priority is being neglected by senior staff members. The meaning of organizational phenomena may also be evident in the jargon and local vocabulary used by members. Nonverbal behavior such as physical gestures, dress patterns, physical arrangements, and office decor can also provide meaningful information (Goffman, 1959; Steele, 1973), provided that the observer is familiar with the context in which this behavior occurs and checks interpretations against other data sources. Although such observational data can be very informative, their reliability is often low, and they are usually hard to quantify.

Assessing the Impacts of Fits

As Figure 3 suggests, consultants should assess the impacts of system fits directly, rather than assuming, as some authors do (e.g., Beer, 1980, Nadler & Tushman, 1980) that high levels of fit or system integration are always preferable. Instead, any particular pattern and level of fit can be assumed to have both costs and benefits that can only be identified and weighed in terms of specific effectiveness criteria (see Chapter 2). For example, gaps between official rules and actual behavior, such as the hoarding of supplies by units on a military base, may cause wastage and raise costs but may also contribute to unit solidarity and morale. In some instances employees may even produce higher quality work by violating official procedures. For instance, Blau (1955, pp. 91–116) reports how group solidarity and work quality were strengthened when employees in a federal agency consulted peers about problems, rather than turning to their supervisors as instructed. As the following discussion on power shows, there are also many instances where unofficial relationships and processes contribute directly to task performance. Hence, practitioners should try to assess the impacts of actual practices directly with clear effectiveness criteria in mind rather than assuming in advance that they are either positive or negative.

The implications of fits between design variables, technologies, and environments also need to be carefully assessed. Consider, for example, the following case:

> Central Acadamy is a small, religiously affiliated private school. It has enjoyed growth in its student body for several decades, is generously supported by a group of donors, and has developed structures, processes, technologies, and an organizational culture grounded in religious teachings that seem to fit well with one another. Conflicts are rare, administration is trouble free, and school-community relations are placid.

In terms of the school's resource position and its internal system states, the fit between system elements is highly effective. On the other hand, the administration and faculty lack new ideas about how to run the school and what programs to develop. Thus, the school may have become incapable of meeting new challenges and opportunities. Like many other organizations, when judged in terms of innovativeness and adaptive capacity, its fits are too high, rather than too low (see Katz & Kahn, 1980, p. 174).

System incongruities and lacks of fits are often necessary for organizational growth and change. Lacks of fit often characterize organizations in which certain parts of the organization or system elements—such as the technology, goals, or human resources—are changing more rapidly than others. In cases like these, the resulting tensions may reflect and even foster creativity, innovation, and adaptation to external change (Burns, 1961: Robbins, 1978). If these states are desired, it would be unwise to try to reverse the technological changes or otherwise force elements into alignment.

Practitioners should also bear in mind that many organizations operate successfully with fairly high levels of structural incongruity and inconsistency. Some "high tech" firms, for example, tolerate overlaps between units, ambiguous definitions of unit goals and assignments, and high levels of infighting and politicking in order to sustain and encourage creativity and initiative (e.g., Kidder, 1981). From one point of view the gaps between official policy and actual practice in educational and service organizations also have positive consequences, as they help their members ward off outside interference (Meyer & Rowan, 1977). In addition, in most types of organizations there seem to be a range of ways in which basic organizational problems may be handled and much room for variation within the recurring organizational types—such as the organic and mechanistic types—observed by consultants and researchers (Van de Ven & Drazin, 1985).

For all of these reasons, consultants should assess system fits and lacks of fit in terms of explicit effectiveness criteria. Then they can decide whether a particular lack of fit is detrimental and what steps, if any, should be taken to improve fits. Consider, for example, the case of the fit between the division's objectives and its reward mechanisms described at the beginning of the chapter: If adaptability to external change was used as the key effectiveness criterion, the consultant and client might legitimately have concluded that managerial behavior should be evaluated over a longer time frame and more emphasis given to planning and management development. In contrast, if satisfying stockholders was used as a key measure of effectiveness, then there might be no choice but to continue linking rewards to short-term results. Management development would continue to be a low priority, whereas responsibility for planning might be assigned to staff specialists, who would not be held responsible for the division's short-term profits.

POWER RELATIONS AND PROCESSES

Power relations and influence processes are among the most important types of actual behavior to examine in diagnosis. Even if an understanding of "political" processes and power distribution does not lead directly to proposals for organizational improvement, it can greatly help consultants manage the consulting process. The following typical "war story" (Quinn, 1977, p. 23) illustrates the potential impact of power on efforts to introduce organizational change:

> In a major textile fibers company there were constant fights between strong managers in the divisions of marketing, production, and research and development. Yet when the creation of product-management teams was proposed in order to "coordinate the very things that caused the friction," the feuding managers formed a powerful coalition to resist the innovation.

The terms *power* and *influence* are used interchangeably in this book to refer to the ability to get people to do things that they might otherwise not do and to the capacity to get things done (Kanter, 1977; Mintzberg, 1983, p. 5). Political actions—attempts to achieve desired outcomes—often aim at influencing budgeting decisions and other forms of resource allocation, at shaping goals and programs, promoting or resisting personnel changes, and at determining the resolution of conflicts and crises (Burns, 1961; Pfeffer, 1981b; Zald & Berger, 1978).

If they understand an organization's power structure and politics, consultants may be able to work in ways that are in keeping with these political realities without compromising the consulting relationship. If they ignore these realities, they are likely to encounter resistance to their diagnoses and may recommend interventions that will have negative consequences or cannot be implemented. In the case cited above, for example, the proposed product management teams would have drawn their members from each of the three functional divisions. But this scheme could only work if the division managers were willing to surrender some of their autonomy. Innovations such as quality circles for production or clerical workers also cannot be implemented successfully unless supervisors and managers are willing to give real power to the members of quality circles. Furthermore, where substantial power differences and fundamental conflicts of interest prevail, many popular organization development techniques—including process consultation (see Chapter 1), Open Systems Planning (see Chapter 5), and team building (Burke, 1982, pp. 258–290; Huse & Cummings, 1985, pp. 113–125)—cannot be used, because they require high levels of trust and interpersonal openness (Huff, 1980; Strauss, 1976; Tushman, 1977).

Diagnosing the Distribution and Uses of Power

Outcomes of influence processes. One problem facing consultants is assessment of the consequences of peoples' efforts to use power to influence others and to attain particular ends. Rather than assuming that any attempt to shape or manipulate others is by definition undesirable, consultants need to acknowledge the essentially political nature of nearly all organizations and look directly at the impacts of influence processes. For example, members may use their power to oppose change, as in the case described above, or they may use it to press for change (Burns, 1961). In many organizations proposals for new products and other innovations only get accepted when powerful managers work hard to convince decision makers to provide the resources needed to develop a new idea and then fight to overcome opposition to its implementation (Kanter, 1983). In some cases such champions of new concepts have even violated official directives and procedures by diverting resources to new product development.

Practitioners can only evaluate such political efforts from the viewpoint of particular actors within the organization and in terms of clear effectiveness criteria. Consider, for example, a situation in which workers marshaled the support of local politicians in order to delay the closing of an unprofitable plant while proposals for keeping the plant going could be reviewed by joint labor-management committees. Consultants to top management who accept their client's concern for profitability would regard the workers as threatening organizational effectiveness. In contrast, a consultant to the workers would probably view their actions favorably (e.g., Alinsky, 1971; Chesler et al., 1978), as might a consultant to management who placed greater stress on job security, plant morale, and the standing of the firm in the community.

Influence tactics. It is important to assess the effects of the tactics people use to influence others, as well as evaluating the outcomes of these efforts. People who have formal authority or control over valued resources may try to influence others and accomplish things by changing the flow of material and social rewards and sanctions to others. Other influence tactics include appealing to logic and common standards, and manipulating people by providing them with selective information about a situation or by creating indirect pressures to act in a particular fashion (Porter et al., 1981). To assess the impacts of such influence tactics and other uses of power, practitioners need to consider issues like these:

—How do those who are subject to a particular influence tactic react to it?
—Does the use of this tactic increase tensions or conflicts between groups?
—Does reliance on personal loyalties or the striking of political deals undercut the organizations's stress on performance or professional excellence?
—Do the methods used to resolve conflicts produce solutions that last and that are regarded as fair?

The power to act. People and groups need power in order to accomplish their tasks and contribute to organizational objectives, as well as to oppose them. A critical question for diagnosis is whether particular groups have sufficient resources and influence to accomplish their tasks. First-line supervisors, for example, often cannot do their jobs adequately because they cannot control or influence the lines of supply to their units, lack vital organizational information, and cannot advance within the organization (Kanter, 1979). Because of their lack of power, the supervisors become resistant to managerial initiatives, administer programs mechanistically, and achieve low productivity. Middle managers also need to acquire power to do their jobs well (e.g., Izraeli, 1975), and staff specialists, like psychologists and planners, often lack both the formal authority and the informal standing needed to get their ideas implemented. Consultants need to be on the lookout for situations like these where group and divisional effectiveness can be enhanced by giving people more control of needed resources and easier access to key decision makers.

Power distribution. Consultants may also approach the question of whether units have enough power by examining the overall power distribution in a division or organization. When power is highly *centralized*, control over important resources and decisions is concentrated in the higher ranks of the organization. Here is a list of possible consequences of shifting toward a more decentralized distribution of authority and power (Carlisle, 1974; Child, 1977; Kanter, 1983; Khandwalla, 1977):

Positive Consequences of Decentralization

Reduced burden on top management to make decisions and process information

Cost savings from reduction in number of levels in the administrative hierarchy

Improved information flow and decision quality

Enhanced ability of middle managers to solve problems on their own

Improved morale

More innovation

Better management development

Negative Consequences

Reduction in top management's ability to forge a unifying strategy for the organization and to shift directions rapidly in response to changes or opportunities

Increased costs for training, compensation, capital equipment, and plant

Duplication of positions

Creation of local power centers

Heightened interunit conflict

To diagnose the distribution of power, practitioners should assess the degree to which the organization is currently decentralized and weigh the probable costs and benefits of changing the current power distribution in the light of explicit effectiveness criteria. Decentralization is more likely to be preferred when high priority is placed on the ability of subunits to respond rapidly and appropriately to local and specialized problems. The need to do so is most likely to arise in very large organizations; those that are geographically dispersed; organizations facing rapidly changing, very complex, or highly competitive environments; and organizations dealing with nonroutine tasks.

INVESTIGATING POWER RELATIONS AND PROCESSES

Indicators of power and influence.[3] Gathering trustworthy information on power relations and processes is a challenge to organizational consultants. First, they need to decide which individuals and groups have acted or might act in ways that could influence the consulting process or the aspects of the organization being studied. In addition to high-ranking managers, there may be interest groups that form along the lines of departments, occupations, ranks, and social characteristics (e.g., sex, ethnic background). Naturally, the actors concerned with one issue, such as the redesign of jobs, may be different than those concerned with another, such as budget allocations. Once key issues and actors have been identified, it is useful to make a chart listing the key actors for each issue, their position on the issue, and their relative power (Pfeffer, 1981 pp. 37–43).

Then practitioners can try to learn how much power various actors have and how they use that power. To do so directly would necessitate following the treatment of specific issues in different parts of the organization and examining political struggles directly. Because this kind of information is rarely available, it is usually necessary to look for overt manifestations of power (Kanter, 1977). Table 7 takes this approach in providing questions on the current state of power relations and suggesting techniques for gathering relevant information. If most of the answers to these questions point to the same groups or individuals, it is very likely that they are indeed the most powerful actors. On the other hand, if some actors appear to be powerful according to one set of criteria (e.g., status symbols) but not according to another (e.g, access to decision-making bodies), investigators will need to obtain additional information in order to determine whether some of the indicators of power are invalid, or whether there are several distinct power bases and no single group of powerful actors.

Data collection techniques. The sensitivity and subtlety of political processes make them hard to measure with questionnaires. Still, some authors have developed questionnaires for identifying powerful groups or individuals, describing prevalent influence tactics, and measuring power distribution (Moch et al., 1983a; Price, 1972; Tannenbaum, 1968; and see the discussions of MOAQ and OAI in

---

3. This section draws substantially on Pfeffer's (1981b, pp. 35–65) discussion of assessing power.

Chapter 3). As Table 7 suggests, a wide range of qualitative and largely unobtrusive techniques can be used as alternatives or supplements to questionnaires.

Some of the strategies and methods listed in Table 7 can also provide data on the uses of power and on its distribution. If practitioners can observe the meetings of major decision-making forums, for example, they may obtain invaluable data on how members resolve differences and conflicts and the degree to which top executives share power with subordinates. Unfortunately, many influence processes occur outside of such formal gatherings and are hard to observe.

TABLE 7
Finding Out Who Is Powerful

Focal Area and Guiding Questions	Research Strategies and Methods
Resources: What kinds of resources are most important to members—funds, equipment, personnel, information, knowledge, and so on. Which groups & individuals get disproportionate shares?	Observe (&/or interview on) key resources and distribution, status symbols; look for disproportionate budget allocations.
Who controls distribution?	Examine organization charts, job descriptions; interview.
Centrality: What technical and administrative processes are vital to everyday operations? What processes are critical to organizational success? Who influences & participates in them?	Interview unit heads; study organization charts, job descriptions; observe operations; analyze reports from interviews and workshops on crises, failures, successes.
Who handles contacts with powerful external groups?	Interview; examine organization charts, job descriptions; survey (i.e., with questionnaires) individuals, unit heads about contacts.
Who is regarded as irreplaceable?	Interview knowledgeable members; survey members of relevant units.

Participation and Influence in Decision Making: Who participates in key (formal and informal) decision-making forums? Who has access to top decision makers?	Examine organization charts, job descriptions, reports on membership in forums; observe participation; interview on access, participation.
Whose views dominated major decisions? Who came out on top in power struggles and conflicts?	Analyze decisions reported in documents, press, interviews, workshops.
Whom do members turn to for help in sponsoring a new idea?	Interview; analyze successes, failures reported in interviews, workshops.
Reputation: Which units and individuals are especially powerful?	Survey members for ranking of influentials; interview; observe attention, deference given to individuals.
Which units do members who want to get ahead join? With whom do they try to develop relationships?	Interview; examine executives' prior positions to find units that are avenues to the top.

To gather data on influence processes, consultants often have to rely on interviews or on discussions during meetings or workshops. In workshops or interviews consultants may ask members to provide detailed accounts of organizational successes, the resolution of past organizational problems and crises, and accounts of the treatment of new ideas or proposals. In providing these accounts, members may, of course, justify and improve upon their own behavior and that of others to whom they are loyal, and they may exaggerate the failings of those they hold in low esteem. Still, when conducted and analyzed with sensitivity to these possibilities, interviews and group discussions can provide insight into members' perceptions of political processes, key political actors, and the kinds of influence tactics in use within the organization. To develop an understanding of power relations and processes that is independent of the perceptions of particular members, practitioners will have to carefully cross-check members' reports with one another and with other kinds of information.

EXERCISES

1. Rewards

Interview the head and at least one subordinate in a department or division. Use a list of guiding, open-ended questions about rewards and their relationships to other features of the unit. In addition to writing questions on your own, you may want to use the following items listed in Appendix A: I-1 & 2; II-1; III-1, 2 & 3; IV-2; VI-1, 2, 5 & 6; VII-1, 2, 3, 6, 7, 8 & 9; VIII-1, 2 & 3; IX-1, 3; XI-1, 2 & 3. Cover the following issues in your interviews and discuss each of them in your report:

(1) What rewards and sanctions (punishments) are widely used?
(2) What kinds of behavior are subject to rewards and sanctions? (be specific)
(3) What types of actions are encouraged and discouraged? Consider hard work versus taking it easy, personal loyalty to supervisors and peers, risk taking, exercising initiative, generating new ideas, cooperation with others in or outside the unit.
(4) Are the same rewards offered to everyone, or can people receive the types of rewards that are more appealing to them? (e.g., one person may want a bonus, whereas the next wants a chance to earn a degree while working.)
(5) How do each of the following influence the current system of rewards—peers, supervisor, higher level management, labor agreements?
(6) If you have sufficient information, assess the fits between the current reward system and the other system elements (see Table 5).

2. Assessing Fits

In this exercise you may draw on your prior knowledge of an organization or gather Basic Organizational Information (see Chapter 2) and then conduct several General Orientation Interviews (Appendix A) before beginning the exercise. Then take a large sheet of newsprint and make a matrix in which all eight of the system elements are listed as rows and columns. Subdivide the resources category further into three categories: people (human resources), knowledge and information, and material resources. If you constructed the matrix correctly, it should be 10 by 10 with 45 cells above the diagonal. Then for each cell ask the following: How well does the row entry (e.g., human resources) fit with the column entry (e.g., knowledge and informational resources)? To make these queries more concrete look at the questions about fit listed in Table 5. Where no question appears in the table, suggest your own. For example, Do the employees (*human resources*) have the *knowledge* needed to perform their tasks or can they readily obtain it? Then make notes on the degree of fit between each pair in your matrix. Be explicit about the criteria you are using for assessing fit. Once you have completed the matrix, note the two cases of poor fit that seem to be most harmful to effectiveness. Be clear about your effectiveness criteria. Write a report on these two relationships in which you explain the nature of the lack of fit, its impacts, and make suggestions for improving the fits.

3. Power to Act

Use at least two of the approaches listed in Table 7 to determine which people have the most power within some subunit of an organization, such as a branch, a division, or a department. Interview two of them about a major problem or challenge facing their unit. Find out during the interview or by some other method whether they have the resources needed to deal with the problem. If not, specify what resources they would need in order to take action and what could be done to help them attain these resources or solve the problem some other way.

5

Diagnosing Environmental Relations

The first part of the chapter shows how to examine the demands and pressures placed on an organization by its environment and how to assess its responses to external conditions. Techniques for conducting intensive interviews are discussed along with other methods for gathering and analyzing data. A discussion follows of Open System Planning, a technique that gives clients most of the responsibility for diagnosing their organization's external relations and for planning appropriate actions.

"High Court to Rule on Job Leaves for Pregnant Workers"
"Citizens' Groups Vow to Defeat Nuclear Dump Proposal"
"IBM Will Enter the Lap-Sized Computer Market"
"$11.7 Billion in Federal Budget Cuts Loom"
"Massive Damage Claims by Former Asbestos Workers"
"Suburbs without Kids! Demand for Family Homes Slumps, Condo Construction Booms"

News items like these remind us daily of the kinds of developments in government, business, technology, and social institutions that can create problems for an organization or pose new opportunities. These external developments can shape the flow of resources to an organization, affect demand for its products and services, and make an impact directly or indirectly on its internal system elements. Naturally, such developments have divergent implications for organizations and stakeholders with divergent interests. State hotel operators, for example, support efforts to block the location of a nuclear dump in the state, whereas members of government agencies and firms developing nuclear power in the region fear that such opposition could lead to industry setbacks. Damage suits against asbestos manufacturers create nightmares for managers in industries where production processes pose health risks. But these corporate liability suits probably encourage workers who face health risks daily, and the growth of such suits opens new markets for the services of legal firms.

This chapter expands the discussion of diagnosing environmental relations begun in Chapters 2 and 4 by providing techniques for diagnosing the responses of a client organization to external conditions and for assessing the organization's strategies for achieving a favorable environmental position. The diagnostic approaches discussed here are usually applied to entire organizations or semi-autonomous divisions but can also be applied to less autonomous units. The less the automony of a focal unit, the more its environment includes other units within the larger organization (e.g., top management) as well as forces beyond that organization's boundary.

GUIDELINES FOR DIAGNOSIS

Diagnosis of an organization's responses to external demands and of its overall relationship to its environment can contribute to managerial decision making or provide a basis for interventions aimed at improving organizational adaptation (see Lauffer, 1977, pp. 47–54 and "Open Systems Planning" below). The key issues in this type of diagnosis are listed here as a set of guidelines for consultants.

(1) *Identify the key conditions in the task environment of the client organization (or unit)—relevant technical and scientific conditions, labor pools, the behavior of competitors, and so on. Describe the external organizations with which the organization interacts—suppliers of resources, consumers of goods and services, supervisory and regulatory groups, unions, competitors, community and political groups having a stake in the organization's actions, and nonmanaging owners (e.g., stockholders).*

The key environmental conditions affecting a manufacturer of microcomputers, for example, include the market for its products, the state of competition within the field, the state of computer technology, and the pool of available talent from which the firm recruits. The external constituencies that have a stake in an organization's affairs and try to influence its operations may include community groups, like those opposing the nuclear dump location, as well as national public interest groups concerned with issues like health, minority employment, and women's issues. Public agencies and service organizations are especially subject to pressures and constraints from external regulatory and certifying bodies (Meyer & Rowen, 1977).

(2) *Describe the nature of the demands and pressures placed on the client organization by the external conditions and organizations and the impacts of these forces.*

Each external group or condition can be thought of as pressing the organization to act in some particular fashion. A city council may be pressing its Youth Services Division to cut back on staff, while community groups are demanding fuller services and greater involvement in decision making. In analyzing external demands, practitioners should describe the degree to which they:

—threaten the flow of needed resources
—disrupt or alter internal operations
—shape receptiveness to organizational outputs

Acquiescence to a demand for community involvement in decision making, for example, would probably require changes in administrative processes and would disrupt current routines. In contrast, external developments may offer *opportunities* for

—expansion or diversification of services or sales
—acquisition of new forms of knowledge or technology
—improvement of political standing and influence over the environment
—recruitment of personnel

Besides examining the specific content of external forces, consultants should also evaluate the degree of *predictability* of important environmental developments. As suggested in Chapter 4, mechanistic administrative procedures can more readily handle predictable environmental developments than rapidly changing, unpredictable ones. One way of assessing environmental predictability is to examine whether the services, work materials, or resources delivered to the environment and received from it during the past year have changed significantly or have remained stable. If they have changed, how well could members of the organization anticipate these changes? Other indications of predictability include the frequency of interruptions, exceptions, and problems associated with obtaining resources such as inputs and delivering goods and services such as outputs (Van de Ven & Ferry, 1980, pp. 141-158).

(3) *Assess the degree to which the client organization depends on the organizations in its task environment.*

The ability of outside groups to influence an organization depends on their authority over that organization's affairs and their control over resources on which the organization is dependent (Pfeffer & Salancik, 1978). In examining external dependencies, consultants should not overlook a client organization's need for public support and approval. These can be as important a resource as cash, personnel, or legal authorization. If decision makers in the client organization can ignore unwanted external demands and continue with "business as usual" without losing public support, they will probably do so.

(4) *Describe how the organization responds to environmental demands and opportunities. Then describe any demands that it places upon its environment as it tries to manage its external relations.*

Practitioners should consider both the concrete actions taken in response to external demands and the implications of these actions for organization-environment relations. For example, the Director of Youth Services could have responded to the demand for greater community participation in decision making by informing the citizens' group that their request was being considered. This response might have reduced external pressure and delayed or avoided the need for a decisive response.

In the short run, organizations can respond to external pressures by using reactive *coping tactics* or they may proactively *intervene* in the environment in order to reduce pressures or shape demands at their source (see Child, 1972; Galbraith, 1977; Miles, 1980; Pfeffer & Salancik, 1978). Here is a list of common *coping tactics* to examine:

—ignoring or evading external demands or pressures
—acceding to those portions of demands that least threaten organizational routines
—adjusting work procedures or flows to take account of changes in the availability of resources or the demand for services
—limiting the impact of pressure groups by assigning responsibility for dealing with them to functions or units (e.g., customer relations) that are isolated from the rest of the organization and have limited impact on it
—monitoring external developments to reduce surprises and disruptions and to facilitate planning

The heads of a junior college, for example, have a variety of options for coping with changes in computer technology and growing student demand for appropriate computer training. They can monitor these developments further by appointing a committee to study the problem, add an introductory course on computers, or incorporate computer skills into existing courses.

In contrast, common ways that organizations may *intervene* in their environments include:

—lobbying and maneuvering for political support
—using economic power to influence external groups (e.g., boycotts, pricing below market to drive out small firms)
—advertising to shape demand or attitudes
—cooperating with other organizations to share resources, reduce competition, and shape other environmental conditions
—creating structural ties with other organizations (contracts, mergers, purchases) that increase control over the environment

(5) *Assess the effectiveness of the organization's coping responses and its interventions in the environment.*

Consultants and their clients should evaluate responses and interventions in terms of agreed-upon effectiveness criteria. In the case of the college, for example, no extra funds were available for computer training, so its costs would have to be balanced by increased revenues. Therefore, adding a course in computers that could attract additional students as well as serving current students was a more effective response from an economic standpoint. Course enrollment fees could generate additional revenues, whereas the purchase of computer equipment for use in existing courses would add expenses without generating revenues.

The Adaptation and Resource Position criteria listed in Table 2 are often used to evaluate organization-environment relations. These criteria emphasize the quality and quantity of resources obtained and the ability of the organization to adapt to external change (see also Chapter 4, "Diagnosing System Fits"). In addition, effectiveness can be defined in terms of the organization's position within its industry and markets and its ability to create favorable external conditions in which to operate.

Consultants may also evaluate the effectiveness of tactics for managing environmental relations in terms of their impact on internal processes. For example, if an organization uses tactics that limit external interference in the work flow, then routines can more readily be established and less expensive and complex forms of coordination can be used (see Chapter 4, "Diagnosing Organization Design").

If external forces create chronic problems and crises, or disruptions periodically reach major proportions, then current responses may be judged to be inadequate. Other signs of ineffective tactics include severe internal tensions and conflicts that result from external pressures, or short-term responses to the environment that create additional organizational problems (see Chapter 2, "Assessing the Feasibility of Change. . . ").

(6) *Identify trends in the general environment that are already affecting the organization or are likely to affect it in the future.*

Changes in the general environment (see Chapter 2), like the legal, social, and political developments illustrated in the news items above, can make current responses outmoded and can present an organization with new problems and opportunities. Many influential developments originate in the general environment and are only felt later in the immediate, task environment. The demand for college courses in computers, for example, reflects changes in the computer industry that have led to the widespread acceptance of computers in the workplace and at home. Some developments in the general environment in areas such as demographics, consumer tastes, life styles, governmental policies, and business cycles may not yet be directly impinging on a client organization, but may be expected to do so in the near future. The declining proportion of suburban families with young children, for example, will eventually show up in declining demand for services to children—such as elementary school education and pediatric medicine—and a growth of demand for adult-oriented services. Practitioners can sometimes help members of an organization anticipate and deal with such important developments. Even though no one can predict external developments with complete certainty, it is usually better to develop plans for dealing with emerging trends than to undergo crises subsequently or miss crucial opportunities.

(7) *Identify alternative responses to the environment that could enhance current or future effectiveness.*

Consultants and clients should first consider whether tactics for coping and environmental intervention might be improved. For instance, a manufacturing firm that is plagued by fluctuations in the price and availability of key raw materials might consider purchasing commodity futures. National parks that suffer from overcrowding during peak season can require campground reservations and restrict access to overcrowded sites in order to spread usage over a wider area.

If effectiveness cannot be achieved by improving coping and external interventions, two types of long-run alternatives can be considered. First, the client organization might *reorganize* by redefining its strategies and goals or by making basic changes in its structure, processes, technology, resource acquisitions and allocations, or even in its culture (see Chapter 4 on possible ways to reorganize). Reorganizations require a significant investment of time and money, and they often have unintended impacts on organizational components that were not direct targets for change. The introduction of new forms of automation in manufacturing, for example, may increase the importance of those functions charged with monitoring and controlling the automated operations and thereby lead to conflicts between this new interest group and older occupational groups. Hence, in considering the possibility of reorganization, consultants need to pay attention to the organization's readiness and capacity for change and should help clients weigh the potential benefits of reorganizations against their potential costs and any likely negative consequences (Chapter 2). A useful way to assess likely consequences is to examine the ways in which reorganizations will affect fits between system elements (see Chapter 4).

A second way that an organization can handle external problems and improve its environmental standing is to *change one or more of its environmental domains*—by entering into a new field or by changing products, services, or markets (e.g., IBM's entry into the lap-sized computer market). The key issue in evaluating such a possibility is whether the shift will strengthen or weaken the organization's *strategic position* (Andrews, 1971; Porter, 1980)—its ability to obtain resources and dispose of outputs on favorable terms. Strategic advantage often derives from the ability to provide a product or service that is superior in price, quality, or terms of delivery than those offered by the competition—or in being their sole supplier. To obtain such an advantage over potential competitors, organizations need to exploit their *distinctive capacities* to the fullest. In the case of the lap-sized computer market, for example, IBM's advantage may stem from its reputation and from the compatibility of the new, portable machines with the personal computer (PC) and other IBM computers. In assessing the possible effects of entering a new domain, consultants will have to rely on estimates by members of the organization or on studies by market researchers or other experts.

It is possible to analyze the strategic position of nonprofit organizations, as well as of businesses. If, for instance, the directors of a new art museum seek to attract donations and public support in a city that already has a well-established art museum, they should try to develop areas of distinctive competence for the new museum. They could, for example, develop collections in areas where the veteran museum has few holdings or provide unique educational services to the public. Although many nonprofit organizations can shift environmental domains, others may be unable to do so because of their charter, public pressures, or their commitments to a particular organizational identity and mission.

DIAGNOSTIC METHODS

Data Gathering

Interviewing. Information about environmental relations is often gathered primarily through interviews with top management and other officials with responsibility for handling external relations (e.g., sales, public relations, customer services, fund-raising) or for monitoring external developments (e.g., long-range planning). The first six entries in the guidelines above give the main issues to cover in an interview on external relations. To prepare questions in advance, a schedule could be created using questions like those shown in sections IV and V of the General Orientation Interview in Appendix A.

Constructing an interview guide. Alternatively, investigators with experience in semistructured interviewing could construct an interview guide (Schatzman & Strauss, 1973). The guide lists all the topics to be investigated and then allows the interviewer to frame each question to reflect the distinctive circumstances of the client organization and take into account previous answers. Interview guides ensure coverage of major topics while allowing flexibility, but they provide for less reproducible results and require more interviewer skill than do more structured schedules. A guide designed to cover the aspects of external relations discussed above might contain the following major headings:

(1)   Key conditions—main markets, fields in which organization operates
(2)   Key outside organizations

(3) Main units, people handling contacts with outside
(4) Demands, pressures from outside; problems, difficulties, opportunities encountered in dealing with environment
(5) Indications of impacts of external forces on dynamics (growth, contraction, adjustments, etc.); effects on internal states (conflict, cohesion, etc.); impacts on resource flows (money, human resources, etc.); organization's level of adaptation to external forces
(6) Responses (coping/intervention) to external problems, demands, and opportunities
(7) External trends that are affecting or may affect organization

Then each major heading in the guide would be broken down into subheadings to cover particular issues. For example, item 6 might be broken down as follows:

(6) Responses to external problems, demands, opportunities
(6a) Specific actions—describe in detail what was done, by whom
(6b) Impact of these responses on external actor (Sample question: "How did x react to the steps you took?")
(6c) Other actions (Interviewer: look for interventions to change external forces versus reactions to pressures—e.g., "Did your group ever make any other attempts to moderate these pressures, deflect these criticisms, anticipate such developments, etc.?")
(6d) Internal impacts (Interviewer: probe for felt effects of tactics, whether they produced desired results, how successful they seem to respondent, and meaning of success for him or her.)
(6e) Changes in tactics and impacts—were similar problems handled in same way in past? (Probe for shifts in tactics, stance toward environment, variations in impacts.)

Naturally, when practitioners conduct interviews with a guide like this, they are prepared for the possibility that the person's answers will range across the topics listed in the guide. During the interview the responses are recorded in the order given. Afterward, to facilitate analysis they can be organized according to the topics in the guide.

Standardized questionnaires. Standardized questionnaires can be used to gather data on external relations if reliable, structured measures are needed to facilitate comparisons between units. To assess the degree to which members of a unit view their environment as unpredictable, heads of units and several subordinates may be asked directly about the nature of external forces, the extent to which they have changed in recent years, their predictability, and the difficulties they pose for conducting the work at hand. (See Lawrence

& Lorsch, 1969, pp. 247–250, for open and closed questions appropriate to manufacturing firms, and Van de Ven & Ferry, 1980, pp.
241–258, for items applicable to both profit-oriented and nonprofit
organizations.) Measures can also be developed of other variables,
such as members' perceptions of environmental competitiveness and
munificence, environmental demands and opportunities, the tactics
used to deal with the environment, and the perceived impacts of these
tactics.

Other data sources. Valuable information about external relations
can also be obtained from the popular press and business-oriented
publications, from information sources like Standard and Poors, and
from organizational documents. Sometimes it is also feasible to
interview members of key external constituencies, such as the head of
an environmental defense group that opposes the expansion of a
client's physical plant. Outside experts on topics like the state of an
industry or technology may also be consulted. Additional data may
come from market studies that were conducted prior to the diagnostic
study. Moreover, if issues of marketing are especially critical to the
diagnosis, consultants may suggest that clients conduct further
market studies before deciding to move into new domains or change
their products or services.

Analysis and Feedback

Data analysis and interpretation. The organization design models
presented in Chapter 4 can provide guides to analyzing the fits
between external conditions and a client organization's structure,
technology, and processes. In particular, practitioners can assess
whether coordination mechanisms are appropriate to the degree of
environmental predictability. Units that face very unpredictable
environments (e.g., customer preferences influenced by sudden
changes in fads and fashions) and those facing poorly understood
conditions (e.g., scientific knowledge about mental illness) will
usually need to make more use of complex, lateral coordination
mechanisms and organic administrative systems.

Another approach to analyzing data on environmental relations
is to examine the extent to which a focal unit uses each of the tactics
listed in number 4 of the guidelines above and to consider the
impacts of commonly used tactics like advertising or seasonal adjustments of the work force. In this way consultants may uncover ways
that current tactics could be made more effective and may discover

neglected possibilities for managing external relations. An additional procedure for mapping external contacts is described in Exercise 1 at the end of this chapter.

Except in very small organizations, each unit in a client organization will deal with a different *subenvironment* consisting of those sectors of the environment most relevant to the unit's operations. In a manufacturing firm, for example, the subenvironment of sales includes customers, the competition, and the pool of potential sales employees. In contrast, production managers will deal with the production technology, the availability of raw materials, suppliers, distributors, unions, and the labor pool of production workers. During analysis of environmental relations in complex organizations, practitioners should construct profiles of the main features of the *subenvironments* of such major units. These profiles should note the following features:

—predictability
—complexity (number of relevant external organizations and degree of difference between them)
—competitiveness
—degree of economic or political threat to unit and the organization as whole
—distinctive problems and challenges posed
—appropriate coping and intervention tactics

Units will have to be organized differently to respond to variations in their subenvironments. The greater the differences between subenvironments, the greater will be the need for differentiation and for complex forms of integration within the organization as a whole.

To make characterizations of the environments faced by an entire organization or division—for example, to determine how threatening or supportive the environment is—practitioners will often have to create a composite picture drawn from the reports of people who are knowledgeable about particular subenvironments. Information on organizationwide impacts of responses to the environment can be synthesized in the same fashion. In addition, to decide which responses to the environment work best, practitioners may be able to compare past responses to current ones, or to contrast the approaches of units facing similar conditions.

Preparations for feedback. Once the consultant has obtained an integrated view of the organization's environment, its current environmental responses, the impact of these responses, the possible ways of improving environmental relations, the findings can be prepared for feedback. Feedback can focus directly on the effectiveness of current relations and ways to enhance effectiveness or it can present findings on the state of the environment and external relations as stimuli for self-analysis and decision making. One important issue to consider in preparing feedback is the extent to which members are correctly reading external conditions and have an accurate picture of their organization's's relationship to the environment. If members are misreading environmental conditions and relations, then judicious feedback of data can help members discover the gap between their perceptions and actual conditions and motivate them to look for ways to improve their monitoring and interpretation of external forces.

Drawbacks of a consultant-centered diagnosis of external relations. Although the approach to data gathering and analysis described here is feasible, it has several drawbacks. First, because the burden for gathering and analyzing the data rests heavily on the consultants, they may be encouraged to draw most of the conclusions about the effectiveness of current responses and available alternatives, without involving organizational decision makers in this interpretive process. If the diagnostic conclusions and recommendations are presented in a finalized fashion, clients and other members are unlikely to identify with them or view them as practical and appropriate (see Chapter 3, "Feedback characteristics"). Skillful consultants can partly overcome this limitation by meeting periodically with clients to discuss their findings and interpret them and by proposing that clients draw the conclusions from the findings.

A second drawback of the consultant-centered approach is that it is time consuming and costly, as only highly skilled interviewers and analysts can gather and interpret the necessary information. Third, there is a risk that the feedback will not seem valid to clients because the data and interpretations do not reflect the clients' own experiences and points of view. Fourth, a consultant-centered analysis of external relations may founder on divergences in members' interests and goals. Feedback from diagnoses of external relations is especially vulnerable to conflicts and ambiguities of this sort, because the diagnosis of external relations usually raises questions about the appropriateness of current strategies and about the fits between an organization's purposes and its responses to the environment. Unless clients can agree on goals and strategies, they are likely to disagree on the implications of the diagnosis and find it impossible to implement its recommendations.

OPEN SYSTEMS PLANNING

Open Systems Planning (OSP) is a client-centered, diagnostic intervention that may help consultants overcome the limitations of a consultant-centered diagnosis of external relations (Beckhard & Harris, 1977, pp. 58–69; Burke, 1982, pp. 65–70; Fry, 1982; Jayaram, 1976.) In OSP, consultants conduct a series of workshops with members of an organization or subunit who have responsibility and authority to engage in planning and to make decisions affecting the organization's strategic relations to its environment. The workshop participants diagnose their organization's current situation and decide what steps to take to deal with external challenges. The consultant facilitates and guides the discussion, records and summarizes it, and gives feedback without dictating the content of the diagnosis and the planning. Groups whose members are familiar with the background and approach of OSP could also use it without the aid of an external consultant. Here is a summary of the main steps in OSP, phrased as a set of instructions to participants:[1]

(1) *Analyze current environmental conditions*—Create a map showing the external conditions, groups, and organizations in the task environment, and the demands, problems, and opportunities created by these forces.

(2) *Analyze current responses to the environment*—Describe the ways in which the organization is currently handling these environmental demands and conditions. All important transactions with the task environment should be considered.

(3) *Analyze actual priorities and purposes*—Define current goals, values, and priorities by examining current responses to the environment and the organization's internal features (structure, processes, culture, etc.). If possible, reach agreement on the organization's current guiding mission.

(4) *Predict trends and conditions*—Predict likely changes in external conditions over the next two to five years. Assess the future of the

1. This summary, which synthesizes and slightly adapts Jayaram's (1976) approach, also draws on Burke (1982, p. 66) and Plovnick et al. (1982, pp. 69–70). The main advantages of Jayaram's approach over that of Beckhard and Harris (1977, pp. 58–69) is that it allows the definitions of purposes and priorities to emerge from the discussions of the current and ideal states, and only requires the achievement of working agreements about operating priorities. This approach to defining goals and priorities seems more realistic than expecting participants to agree in advance on the organization's core mission (see Fry, 1982).

organization if it maintains its current responses to the environment.

(5) *Define an ideal future*—Create scenarios for an ideal future state. These scenarios can envision changes in the organizational purposes and priorities, in external conditions, and in responses to the environment.

(6) *Compare current and ideal states*—In light of projected trends (step 4), define gaps between current and ideal future states in purposes, external conditions, and organizational responses. These gaps may be thought of as differences between where the organization seems to be going and where you want it to be.

(7) *Establish priorities*—Assign priorities to the gaps between ideal and current conditions. Define areas of working agreement and identify disagreements about values, priorities, and purposes.

(8) *Plan appropriate actions*—Plan ways of moving toward agreed-upon future states by narrowing the most important gaps identified in stages 6 and 7. Plan immediate actions and those that will be undertaken after six months and two years. Consider actions for resolving disagreements. Create a schedule for following up on actions and updating plans.

OSP requires participants to use constructive problem-solving techniques to discover and deal with differences in their priorities and objectives. As Jayaram notes, this approach can only work well where members trust and cooperate with one another. If participants can reach a working consensus on ideal future states, they may be able to use OSP successfully to assess the organization's current strategic stance toward its environment and to plan changes in this stance (see Beckhard & Harris, 1977, for examples). An additional requirement for the effective use of OSP is that participants must have the power to put their plans into action (see Chapter 4). Otherwise, the whole process will become an exercise in frustration that may ultimately alienate and embitter participants. To conduct OSP, consultants need to be highly skilled in working with groups in training-type situations, as well as having diagnostic skills.

EXERCISES

1. **External Contacts**
    Based on information gathered in previous exercises or on your own involvement in an organization, choose a unit within an organization that has substantial external contacts (both within and beyond the organization's boundaries). Interview the head of the unit using

parts IV and V of the General Orientation Interview in Appendix A. Make a chart showing the focal unit at the center and all the other units and groups around it. Then color code the chart to show the external groups or units on which the focal unit is most dependent for resources or services, the ones with which contact is most frequent, and any outside units that have authority over the focal unit. Describe the routines and procedures linking the focal unit to two of the most important external units and indicate how these procedures could be improved or how relations with these important units could be improved through other means. (For additional, related exercises see Lauffer, 1977, pp. 50-51; 1982, pp. 30-42.)

2. **Diagnosing External Relations**

   Construct a detailed interview guide that reflects the issues raised in the Guidelines for Diagnosis given above. Using this guide, interview the head of a unit or small organization. Organize the responses to the interview and your conclusions about it in terms of the categories given in the guidelines.

6

Challenges and
Dilemmas of Diagnosis

Practitioners of diagnosis may seek ways to solve specific problems, or they may aim higher—at discovering enduring ways to improve organizational effectiveness or at promoting organizational learning. This chapter examines ways in which practitioners can manage the consulting practice to promote such higher-level goals and to make their work as useful as possible to clients. Then it examines ways of dealing with some of the recurring ethical and professional dilemmas that arise during organizational diagnosis.

The preceding chapters focused on diagnostic processes, interpretations, and methods. The examination of each of these facets of diagnosis raised somewhat different issues for the practitioner. *Process* issues concern the relationships that develop between consultants and clients. *Interpretive* issues include the definition of diagnostic problems and the interpretation of findings. *Methodological* issues relate to the techniques for gathering, summarizing, and analyzing data. Chapter 1 introduced all three kinds of concerns. Chapters 2 through 5 presented diagnostic models that can guide interpretation, methods for applying them, and related process issues.

Despite their usefulness, the models discussed in this book and others like them cannot serve as step-by-step guides to diagnosis. Nor can they be used like equations into which bits of data can be inserted in order to produce a completed assessment. No such recipes for diagnosis or for action planning exist, and none is likely to be discovered. Instead, these interpretive models can serve as accounting schemes and guides to help both experienced and would-be practitioners sort out what is going on within an organization. A further limitation of these models is their selective emphasis on particular organizational phenomena. Some focus mainly on one level of analysis (individual, small groups and units, or the total organization), and all stress certain organizational features more than others. Only by combining these partial views and shifting back and forth between them can practitioners deal with the multifaceted nature of modern organizations.

Anyone who undertakes a diagnosis thus faces many choices as to which models and methods to use and how to manage the consulting process. In most cases each available alternative has some advantages and some drawbacks. Frequently the emerging relationship between clients and practitioners and practical considerations, such as the accessibility of data, have a decisive influence on the choices among alternatives. Although we have referred throughout the book to these choices and have suggested issues to consider in making them, would-be practitioners will need firsthand experience in diagnosis and consulting processes, along with further training in organizational analysis and research methods, to develop the ability to make these judgments themselves (see Appendix C).

This chapter seeks to place these immediate choices within the context of the larger challenges and dilemmas facing practitioners of diagnosis. The first part of the chapter discusses five possible goals for diagnosis and some of the requirements for attaining these goals. The second part deals with ethical and professional dilemmas that often confront practitioners.

A successful diagnosis can sometimes contribute directly to organizational improvement or provide the foundations for a program of organization development. Still, even successful studies may make only modest contributions and may serve the needs of powerful clients more than those of other members of the client organization. Even to achieve these limited ends, practitioners must be as attentive to considerations of consulting process as they are to methods of collecting and analyzing data and to models of organizational functioning.

CHALLENGES OF DIAGNOSIS

Diagnostic Goals

The goals toward which consultants and clients may aspire when planning a diagnosis form a hierarchy.[1] Higher-level goals envision more significant and durable impacts on the organization than lower-level ones. Achieving higher-level goals also requires the consultant to be more skilled in managing the consulting process and requires stronger client commitments. Consultants and clients often

---

1. This section applies and adapts Turner's (1982) discussion of consulting goals.

begin their relationship by defining lower-level goals and gradually adopt a higher-level goal as the consulting relationship evolves. The following discussion presents these goals in ascending order.

(1) Provide specific information or evaluation. The most modest goals involve providing specific information to clients (e.g., public satisfaction with automatic teller machines) or evaluating operations according to clearly defined standards (e.g., determining whether day care programs enable mothers to go to work). Strictly speaking, gathering and reporting such specific information are not forms of diagnosis, as defined in this book. This informational goal is noted here because discussions between clients and consultants about such fact-finding studies often lead to the negotiation of diagnostic goals. Before agreeing to gather specific information, practitioners should try to clarify what clients will do with the information and why they need it. Sometimes clients ask for very specific data on the assumption that the data will help them resolve more general problems or improve organizational functioning. In these cases the practitioner may suggest that a higher-level, diagnostic goal would more accurately reflect the clients' needs.

(2) Solve a specific problem. Clients often seek help in handling specific problems, such as turnover or public dissatisfaction with an organization's services. Sometimes clients' descriptions of problems pin the blame on specific people or groups. In attempting to understand and discover possible solutions to the problems presented by clients, practitioners may discover more general states of which the presented problems are symptomatic. Thus, practitioners should examine ways in which the problems have been handled in the past, groups and relationships that are linked to the problems, and the clients' ability to implement steps that might help solve their problems. In exploring these issues consultants and clients may redefine presented problems in terms of broader problems or challenges, or they may redefine the goal of the relationship as a general assessment of organizational effectiveness.

(3) Assess organizational effectiveness. In this book, we have treated the assessment of effectiveness and the discovery of routes to its improvement as the central goals of diagnosis. Some diagnostic studies assess current effectiveness but leave the discovery of routes to improvement up to the clients. Even studies of this type may contain some implications for action in the very selection of the factors that are examined and reported upon. Whether or not the report on the study includes recommendations, it must use clearly defined criteria of organizational effectiveness (see Chapter 2).

(4) Recommend ways to improve effectiveness. Clients who request assessments of effectiveness typically also want to receive recommendations for improving effectiveness. The search for ways to improve operations requires consultants and their clients to identify the causes of effectiveness and ineffectiveness and to find ways in which clients can intervene (with or without the help of practitioners) to improve current functioning. Most interventions concentrate on changing one or more of the major system elements, such as structures, strategies (purposes), people (human resources), or processes (see Chapter 1, "Organization development interventions"; Chapter 2, "The System . . ."). As they consider routes to improvement, consultants should bear in mind that there may be several alternative ways of intervening to produce a particular result.

The choice of which interventions to recommend and the clients choice of which, if any, to implement will depend on the following considerations (see Chapter 2, "Assessing the Feasibility of Change. . . "):

(1) Diagnostic findings about problems and workable solutions
(2) Available resources—including the skills of consultants and members who are to be involved in the implementation
(3) Anticipated costs
(4) Likely effects—possible benefits versus possible negative consequences
(5) Members openness to various interventions
(6) Support for the interventions by members responsible for implementation and powerful members of the organization

Consultants and clients must therefore weigh the potential costs and benefits of any intervention carefully before planning to implement them. Consider, for example, the use of workshops and training sessions to teach people the concepts and interpersonal skills necessary for teamwork in committees and project groups. These interventions require substantial investments of time but may have very limited or temporary impacts, unless they are accompanied by changes in organizational structures and processes (Katz and Kahn, 1978). On the other hand, structural reorganizations—such as the restructuring of coordination procedures or the redesign of reward patterns—are also expensive and often have unintended consequences. Structural changes are likely to be resisted if they do not fit the prevailing beliefs and norms within the organizational culture and if they conflict with the ways in which people are accustomed to working with one another.

(5) Contribute to organizational learning. In the long run organizational effectiveness—no matter how it is defined—depends on the ability of members to adjust to future states and solve problems that have not yet arisen. Consultants seek to promote organizational learning in order to contribute to the capacity of client organizations to deal with challenges and problems that lie in the unforeseen future (Argyris and Schon, 1978; Hedberg, 1981; Turner, 1982). *Organizational learning* refers to changes in the body of interpretations and accepted responses that guide members in their treatment of problems and challenges. It involves two separate processes—learning by individual members of an organization, and the incorporation of new understandings and directives for action into the organization. Past understandings and responses to problems are embedded in many aspects of the organizational structure, including:

—rules and standard operating procedures
—assignments of jobs and responsibilities
—control procedures
—reward systems

Past interpretations and accepted categories for analyzing problems are also stored in the organizational culture in such forms as

—symbols, terminology, jargon, and stereotypes
—myths and stories about past successes and failures
—widely accepted beliefs about the organization and its environment

Suppose, for example that consultants help an international corporation develop ways to monitor and analyze potentially threatening political events in developing countries as a guide to making investment decisions. The firm can only be said to have *learned* to use this new approach when procedures for conducting political analysis have become an established and influential part of its planning and decision making. When the concepts and images from these new analyses start to pepper the lunch conversations and the more formal deliberations of top executives, the new approach is starting to penetrate the organizational culture.

Organizational learning is needed when environmental and technological conditions are changing substantially and the existing repertoire of responses is becoming incomplete or inadequate (see Chapters 4 and 5). Even if external and technological conditions remain stable, learning is needed to improve the ways in which the organization deals with them. Organizational learning can lead to *small adjustments* within the bounds of current routines or to *significant reorganizations* of the ways members think about their organization and its environment. In contrast to modest adjustments, learning that results in basic changes in structures, processes, technologies, and other system elements requires the *unlearning* of previous responses and the introduction of new behavior patterns. Unfortunately, many structural, interpersonal, and psychological forces resist such basic learning. Even rarer and more difficult to accomplish are fundamental revisions of the underlying theories or models that members use to interpret their organization and its environment. Major crises or imposed reorganizations are usually prerequisites to such radical transformations of an organization's culture.

Making Diagnosis Useful:
The Role of Process

Successful management of the consulting process is necessary for the achievement of even the lower-level, more modest diagnostic goals and becomes all the more complex and critical as diagnostic goals become more ambitious. Here are some of the main features of the consulting process that affect the ability to attain diagnostic goals.

Providing useful feedback. Although feedback is important for all levels of diagnosis, it is especially critical for studies that include recommendations for improving effectiveness or that seek to promote organizational learning. A primary requirement for feedback is that it be valid and relevant to the recipients (Argyris, 1970). No matter what their goals, practitioners should exercise care to provide valid, accurate feedback. The validity of feedback on the organization's current state can be checked by independent investigations by members or practitioners, and by generating predictions from the feedback. In addition to being valid, feedback must be intelligible and meaningful to recipients. Recipients may ignore or reject feedback that is too technical or too distant from their everyday concerns and experiences.

To make feedback useful practitioners need to pay close attention to its motivational implications (Block, 1981; Nadler, 1977). For example, feedback that explicitly compares the performance of units can help motivate action by showing that some people have overcome obstacles facing the client group and have achieved greater effectiveness. This approach reduces the tendency for recipients of the feedback to feel that nothing can be done and may point the way toward workable solutions. Similarly, feedback that points toward attainable ends is more motivating than feedback that sets goals too far beyond the current state or suggests that members must totally transform themselves or their organization (see Chapter 3, "Feedback," for other characteristics of feedback that enhance motivation).

Fostering commitment and ownership of findings and recommendations. As consultants pursue higher-level diagnostic goals, they need to invest increasing efforts in insuring that clients become committed to feedback and to proposals for intervention. The best way to foster commitment of this sort seems to be to involve those members who will have to implement recommendations as fully as possible in all stages of the diagnosis (see Chapter 1, "Participation in Diagnosis. . . ."). Sometimes practitioners encourage involvement of this sort by asking that a liaison group be formed within the client organization which will take an active part in the study. Encouraging members to engage in self-diagnosis is another approach to enhancing commitment to diagnostic findings and interpretations. Even if they cannot participate actively in the diagnosis itself, members who will have to act on its findings should be encouraged to decide themselves what to do about the results, rather than having recommendations pressed upon them by the consultant or by their supervisors (Argyris, 1970). Although these more client-centered approaches to diagnosis can lead to findings and engender commitment to them, these approaches are not suitable for every diagnostic study. Practitioners must be careful to use a consulting style that will fit the culture and expectations of the client organization and that reflects their own training and disposition.

Most diagnoses threaten the interests of at least some members of the focal organization, but practitioners can heighten members' responsiveness to the study by moderating such personal threats whenever possible. In particular, they can make it clear to all participants that they will not make recommendations concerning the placement or retention of individuals and will not report any findings about specific people. Although this approach can increase trust and cooperation, it often cannot be applied to heads of units, who are closely identified with the unit's operations and are held responsible for them by management.

Identifying feasible solutions and interventions. Close contact with knowledgeable and influential members of the client organization can substantially increase consultants' ability to develop workable recommendations for change and can heighten internal support for the diagnosis and its findings. Hence, if consultants work with a liaison group, they should be sure that the group includes influential members of the organization and is not entirely composed of members of advisory units (such as personnel and planning), who may lack influence and inside information. Unless practitioners become aware of the political realities of the client organization early in the diagnostic engagement and actively deal with these realities, they are likely to find that their feedback and recommendations are dismissed by decision makers as irrelevant or unworkable (see Chapters 2 and 4). Even if practitioners do try to take account of political realities, resistance to change may be overwhelming.

Helping clients develop the capacity for self-examination and problem solving. To promote organizational learning consultants must help members view themselves and their organization objectively and develop the capacity for self-examination. To promote learning diagnosis needs to surface hidden assumptions and approaches to problem solving, negative information, conflicts, dilemmas, and basic approaches and routines that are built into the organization's structure and culture. One way consultants can help members surface their hidden interpretations is to give them a limited amount of descriptive feedback, encourage them to analyze these data, and then help them see what assumptions they made as they were analyzing the data.

In addition, to promote problem solving and testing of assumptions by members, consultants can encourage members to develop models or hypotheses about the way their organization is operating, to test them against reality, and to reformulate them accordingly (Schon, 1983). Consider, for example, the division head who received feedback that linked a lack of planning among division managers to a reward system that stressed short-term performance (see Chapter 4). The division head could have been encouraged to test the hypotheses that the reward system was causing the neglect of planning by looking at managerial behavior in units in which planning and longer-term results *were* rewarded. To encourage this kind of problem solving, consultants need to take on a *facilitative*, reflective role, rather than that of the *expert*, who supplies clients with completed solutions to their problems. Diagnostic interventions like Open Systems Planning (Chapter 5) seek to develop this kind of self-understanding and to foster new forms of problem solving. Interventions that promote periodic self-study and evaluation are another way of encouraging organizational learning (e.g., Nadler et al., 1976; Torbert, 1981; Wildavsky, 1972).

In summary, adequate diagnosis is a necessary, but not a sufficient condition for promoting effectiveness and organizational learning. In addition, members of the client organization must deal constructively with the diagnostic feedback, plan appropriate actions, and implement them successfully. Developing these critical links between diagnosis and action is central to organizational consulting but lies beyond the practice of diagnosis itself.

ETHICAL AND PROFESSIONAL DILEMMAS

As the preceding discussion suggest, the role of the practitioner of organizational diagnosis contains many ambiguities and internal tensions (Mirvis and Seashore, 1980). Moreover, there are many possible conflicts between practitioners and members of the client organization. These conflicts and ambiguities can create serious ethical and professional dilemmas for both in-house and external practitioners of diagnosis. Whether or not they are aware of it, as they carry out their work and negotiate their relationships with members of a client organization, consultants are opting for particular resolutions of these dilemmas. The following discussion raises some of these issues in order to help readers better understand diagnosis and prepare to confront these dilemmas in their own work.[2]

Who Benefits?

The sponsors and beneficiaries of diagnosis. No matter how cooperative the relationships between groups within a client organization, some groups and individuals will benefit from a diagnostic study more than others, and some may actually suffer in consequence of it. People who sense that they stand to gain will applaud and support the decision to conduct a diagnosis, whereas those who expect to lose from it will understandably oppose the study. Diagnostic findings may also support certain value positions at the expense of others. For instance, behavioral science practitioners often recommend increas-

2. The following discussion of professional dilemmas draws on Walton and Warwick (1973). See also Bowen (1977) and O'Conner (1977).

ing members' participation in decision making. But this proposal may clash with the values of those who currently hold positions of authority.

Thus, consultants need to consider whether they can legitimately promote certain interests and values at the expense of others. This issue is illustrated by questions like these:

—Are consultants responsible for weighing the conflicting interests and values within an entire organization, or is this solely the job of management?

—Should consultants be willing to have their findings feed into internal political struggles?

—Are consultants supposed to promote the narrow interests of the client who originally sponsored the study, or should they try to help "the whole organization"; some broad stratum within it, such as top management; or all the members of the group whose problems were initially presented?

An additional dilemma arises when consultants discover that they cannot identify personally with the goals or the behavior of their clients or other members of the client organization. External consultants can, of course, decline assignments when the client has prejudged the results of the study and plans to use it to justify getting rid of someone or to make some other change. Similarly, external consultants may decline to accept assignments when the organization's mission, goals, culture, or practices directly clash with their own personal values. But what are internal consultants to do about such dilemmas, and what should consultants do when they realize during a study that their findings will encourage behavior that they cannot condone personally or professionally?

Power and politics. Closely related to these issues are those concerned with the role of diagnosis in organizational politics. The mere process of providing people with additional information and understanding of parts of their organization may increase their power. Moreover, a study's recommendations may directly or indirectly enhance the influence and resources of some members or units, at the expense of others. There may also be hidden power implications in the ways in which clients and practitioners define problems and selectively focus on some organizational levels or features (e.g., motivational problems among workers versus structures and managerial styles that affect motivation). At the very least, practitioners should be aware of the power implications of their behavior and should not allow abstract terms like organizational health, system needs, and effectiveness to mask the power trade-offs that are inevitable by-products of diagnosis and intervention.

Top managers are usually the dominant clients for diagnostic studies. Practitioners should ask themselves whether—from the standpoint of their own values and from the standpoint of organizational functioning—they want their work to further enhance the power of those who are already powerful. Some authors (e.g., Alinsky, 1971; Chesler et al., 1978) have responded to the inequalities of power distribution by advocating the use of behavioral science knowledge to assist less powerful groups, such as tenants' unions and block associations in slums. But these change agents do not usually gain sufficient access to the organizations they want to influence to be able to conduct diagnostic studies.

To reduce unforeseen political consequences of their work, practitioners can contract with clients on how diagnostic data will be used. In general it is best if clients do not use diagnostic data to evaluate individual members. Consultants can also try to avoid assignments where the client seems to want to use the study for political purposes—for instance, to diffuse criticism by showing higher-level managers or subordinates that "the issues are being studied." Consultants may also seek to moderate the effects of power struggles by encouraging members to deal with feedback in a spirit of trust and by emphasizing common, nondivisive interests. But consultants can never be certain that some of the recipients of feedback will not react defensively or vindictively to feedback or try to use the findings to enhance their own power at the expense of others.

Implications for individual members. Practitioners also need to confront questions about the privacy and well-being of individual participants in a diagnosis. When employees are told to cooperate with a study even though its findings may be harmful to them, practitioners cannot honestly describe participation as voluntary or as benifiting all members equally. An additional problem involves preserving the privacy and confidentiality of participants.

Naturally, every effort should be made to ensure that none of the data or findings are used in such a way that the opinions or actions of individuals become known. Even if appropriate precautions are taken, the data may still have negative implications for the heads of units, and clients may demand that data relevant to specific individuals be shown to them. Although it is legitimate to refuse to provide such data if the initial agreement ruled out its use, consultants have very little control over what members do with the reported findings. The head of a unit who receives negative feeback from his or her subordinates may punish them for their honesty.

Although there is no way to avoid the ethical dilemmas posed by such possibilities, practitioners can moderate them somewhat by not misrepresenting the purposes and sponsorship of the study and by avoiding manipulative forms of questions and measurement, such as projective tests, that make it difficult for participants in a study to figure out what the investigator really wants to know. Consultants should understand and may even sympathize with participants who are reluctant to expose themselves to criticism or threats to their jobs. On the other hand, consultants should weigh such sympathies with reluctant participants against the responsibility to provide clients with valid and useful diagnostic findings.

Some solutions. Underlying many of the issues discussed so far is the possibility of conflict between clients' interests and those of other members of the organization. Consultants have worked out a variety of solutions to this critical dilemma, ranging from client-oriented to member-oriented.[3] At one extreme lies the Machiavellian view that practitioners of diagnosis, like other types of consultants, owe their loyalties entirely to their clients, who sponsored the diagnosis, judge its outcomes, and are often responsible for paying for it. From this point of view, consultants are absolutely obligated to gather the data and provide the interpretations needed to further their clients' needs. Aside from the serious ethical limitations inherent in this position, it is often unworkable. In practice, it is often very hard to determine who is the client to whom the consultant owes this total loyalty. Is it the person who authorized payment for the study, the individuals who first asked for it, those who approved and sponsored it, or those who will receive the feedback and act on it? In many cases these are quite different people, with divergent needs and interests.

Diametrically opposed to the Machiavellian position is the view that has dominated much of the organization development litera-ture: Consultants are obligated to strive for the improvement of the

3. As the Machiavellian and organization development views described here are ideal types, authors who hold these views are not identified. The former approach dominates much of the writing by instructors in business schools and by management consultants, who often think of consultants as aides to top executives. The organization development view dominated much of the applied work of psychologists and specialists in organizational behavior until the late 1970s and is still prevalent today.

organization as a whole, not to enhance the position of individuals within it. From this vantage point the goals of diagnosis and intervention are the ultimate improvement of organizational properties such as health, effectiveness, cohesion, and so on. This comforting approach solves the dilemmas of power and politics by denying that they exist. Its advocates overlook the realities of differences of interest and talk of abstract organizational needs and states, without recognizing that organizations are composed of individuals and groups who often do not agree on what is good for the system.

Between these two extremes are several approaches that seek to cope more realistically and directly with the essentially political character of organizations. One approach is to seek broad sponsorship and supervision for a diagnosis, so that the members of the organization take on the responsibility for negotiating and resolving many of the power implications of the study. In the Michigan Quality of Work Life project, for example, consultants work with a committee composed of representatives of management and labor (Mirvis & Seashore, 1980). This committee is responsible for reviewing problems and change opportunities and for initiating actions and solutions.

Bowen (1977) has offered a way of relieving consultants of power dilemmas and other conflicts that turns on the definition of the goals of the consultation. Following Argyris (1970) he suggests that the main obligation of consultants is to provide clients with valid information and to allow them the freedom to decide whether or not to take action. This approach has the virtue of discouraging consultants from trying to impose their values on the client organization and encouraging them to accept the fact that power and responsibility for acting on diagnostic findings lies with the members of the organization and not with the consultant. On the other hand, Bowen does not sufficiently specify what constitutes valid information or who the real clients are. His approach may thereby encourage consultants to underestimate the impacts of their own behavior on the organization and to blame clients for failure to enact recommendations.

A less elegant but more realistic solution acknowledges that consultants are responsible to one or more clients and that they must work out a way of handling members' conflicting expectations about their work.[4] Once the priorities of the study and the clients' effectiveness criteria have been clarified (see Chapter 2), practitioners can

---

4. Thanks to my wife, Jo Ann, who helped me work out this solution.

introduce other criteria that are compatible with client goals. In addition, practitioners may try to define problems and look for solutions that avoid divisive, win-lose outcomes that can only benefit one party at the expense of another. Instead they may seek to promote gains for all or most interest groups. As they define problems and seek solutions that will benefit the broadest range of constituencies, rather than generate conflict, consultants can select appropriate effectiveness criteria within the *range* of criteria that are acceptable to powerful clients. Finally, this approach recognizes that consultants may advocate particular priorities and effectiveness criteria, but that they do not always succeed in convincing members to adopt them. Like Bowen's approach, this solution suggests that the members of the organization have the ultimate responsibility for interpreting diagnostic feedback, for deciding what actions are warranted, and for implementing any interventions.

Professional Standards and Responsibility

A somewhat separate set of dilemmas relate to consultants' needs to retain professional standards in the face of the pressures of the consulting practice. First, there is the risk that the need to maintain credibility in the eyes of clients will clash with the dictates of professional honesty. For example, practitioners sometimes find themselves forced to decide whether to risk using new and untested models and techniques or to rely on familiar diagnostic procedures that will provide quick, impressive results but do not entirely fit the diagnostic questions or promote a positive consulting relationship. In like manner, practitioners may feel that they will appear ignorant in the eyes of their clients if they admit that certain organizational problems lie outside of their specialization. But, in fact, many important issues will lie far beyond the competencies of consultants trained mainly in the social and behavioral sciences.

A related difficulty stems from the tentative and ambiguous nature of behavioral science data and findings. As researchers, practitioners are aware that using a different measurement technique or a slightly different definition of the variables might have produced different results. They also realize that issues can be framed in a variety of ways, and that there is more than one plausible interpretation of the state of an organization and the ways to improve it. Can consultants explain such ambiguities to members of the client organization, without making themselves look amateurish and unprofessional? The answer to this question depends on the ways that they define their relationships with clients.

If consultants present themselves as science-based experts who possess all the knowledge and the tools needed to find a solution to any organizational problem, they will have difficulty admitting to such ambiguities. On the other hand, they may acknowledge that both consulting and management are professions that must cope with high levels of *ambiguity and complexity* (Weick, 1979). Both managers and consultants can respond to these challenges by continually formulating, checking, and reformulating interpretations and explanations (Schon, 1983). From this vantage point, consultants should encourage clients to confront ambiguities head on by adopting an *experimental attitude*—"We seem to have a good understanding of what is causing that problem and some good ideas about what to do about them. Let's try them out to see what will happen."

Experiments of this sort can range from systematic tests of the effects of interventions, to less rigorous pilot projects, and to an experimental hypothesis-testing approach to daily affairs. This experimental attitude is illustrated by the manager who has heard about the benefits of delegating authority and decides to test out the theory by encouraging subordinates to assume greater responsibility. Then the manager examines the ways that delegation is affecting the subordinates and their relationships to the manager. In light of this assessment, the manager then adjust his or her subsequent behavior accordingly.

A second dilemma related to professionalism is that a diagnosis that is highly competent from a research standpoint may be counterproductive in terms of its ability to foster clients' receptivness to feedback and commitment to action. The very techniques of data gathering and analysis that spell competence in the eyes of researchers may make particpants in a diagnosis feel anxious and cut off from the study. More client-centered approaches avoid this danger but often have to rely on less sophisticated and less rigorous methods of data gathering and analysis (see Chapter 1).

A third dilemma centers on the evaluation of diagnostic studies. One difficulty is that objective measures of results are often unobtainable. Diagnosis is only one step in a chain of actions that must be completed if effectiveness is to be enhanced. Thus, diagnosis often cannot be evaluated in terms of direct impacts on organizational effectiveness. The task of evaluating a diagnosis is further complicated by the requirement that consultants cannot reveal privileged information about clients and their organizations. Yet evaluation by outside investigators along with criticism and review by peers are needed for objective evaluation and can greatly contribute to the improvement of diagnostic practice. Practitioners can partially compensate for these weaknesses by conducting their own evaluations. In addition, they may publish accounts of their work in which they disguise the identities of client organizations and deal with the abstract, generic significance of their research and experience (Argyris, 1970).

Criteria for evaluating a diagnosis that can be derived from the diagnostic goals discussed above include:

(1) the perceived usefulness of the diagnostic information to clients and other members
(2) the extent to which the diagnosis helped clients and members solve specific problems
(3) the contribution of the diagnosis to members' assessment of their organization's effectiveness
(4) the perceived usefulness of recommendations for improving effectiveness
(5) the degree of use of the diagnostic feedback in decision making and action planning

A fourth dilemma involves conflicts between personal or professional interests and those of clients. University-based consultants, for instance, may be tempted to exploit client organizations as research sites. Similarly, consultants may undertake studies that will pay well, even though it is clear that the client organization is unlikely to use the diagnostic feedback constructively. In both instances, the same kinds of standards that apply to other consulting professions seem to be appropriate here: Practitioners should be encouraged to publish reports of their experiences and findings, and no one would have them take vows of poverty before entering the profession. But they cannot legitimately pursue personal gain in ways that harm their clients or generate unjustified, hidden costs.

CONCLUSION

This chapter has sought to convey some of the crucial challenges and dilemmas facing practitioners of organizational diagnosis. It has emphasized the relationships that develop during the diagnostic process between practitioners, clients, and other members of the client organization. In diagnosis, as in other forms of consultation (Turner, 1982), the ability of practitioners to contribute to organizational improvement depends heavily on the ways they handle these relationships, as well as on their methodological and interpretive expertise.

Practitioners of diagnosis must therefore engage in an elaborate balancing act. They must balance the needs and desires of their clients against those of other stakeholders in the organization and their own professional understandings of organizational effectiveness. They must also balance the requirement for valid, believable data and interpretations against the constraints placed on their time and their resources and the need to generate commitment and openness to the study's findings.

These then, are some of the challenges of diagnosis: To find out what is going on and why, while engaged in a complex and dynamic set of interpersonal relationships. To find a way of serving clients who may be ambivalent about being helped and to deal with people who may be dead set against the consultation. To sort between the constraints of the moment and professional and personal standards. To draw upon a broad range of academic and interpersonal skills in order to provide useful knowledge.

APPENDIX A

GENERAL ORIENTATION INTERVIEW

The orientation interview provides data on the important features
of a department or unit and any problems it is experiencing.[1] Orientation interviews are usually conducted after the practitioner has
obtained basic descriptive data (See Chapter 2, "Basic Organizational
Information"). If such information is lacking or greater depth is
needed on the organization or the division as a whole, the following
interview can be adapted so as to apply to the total organization or
some major division within it. Additional questions can then be
added about the major differences within the organization. The
interview is divided into labeled sections to show the main system
features covered and the levels of analysis (see Chapter 2). The order
and wording of the questions should be modified to fit the organization and to allow the interviewer and respondent to move comfor-
tably from one topic to another. Moreover, interviewers should feel
free to drop questions on issues that respondents have already
covered in their previous answers or to modify questions in light of
earlier responses. An orientation interview can last from 30 minutes
to up to 2 hours. The starred items can be left for subsequent interviews or covered by other forms of data gathering if time is short or
respondents seem uncomfortable with sensitive issues.

Before starting, the interviewer should explain that the purpose of
the interview is to learn about what it is like to work in the unit and
explain who is sponsoring the study (e.g., division management, with
the approval of the union). The interviewer can then explain how the
respondent was selected (at random, by recommendation, because of
his or her position), and state that each person's answers are confidential and that only general summaries of the results will be
revealed (see Chapters 2 and 3 on analysis and feedback).

---

1. This interview draws in part on Burke (1982, pp. 200–202), Levinson (1972, pp.
   527–529), Nadler (1977, pp. 187–191). For additional interviewing guides see
   Kotter (1978, pp. 91–99) and Levinson (1972, pp. 55–65).

GENERAL ORIENTATION INTERVIEW

I. The Person and His or Her Job (Individual Level)

1. What do you do here? Please tell me about your past experience in the organization and your current job. (Probe for job title, description of work, department, or unit in which person works, previous positions in organization, time spent in them.)

2. What is it like to work here? (Probe for feelings about work and atmosphere, e.g., fun, frustrating, competitive.)

II. Work Roles, Technology, and Outputs (Individual and Group Levels)

1. What tasks does your unit (group, department, division) perform? What are the main techniques and means used to do these things?

2. What are the main outputs of this unit—products, services, ideas? What units in the organization or outside it receive these output?

3. How does your job fit into the work done here? With whom do you have to work (inside and outside the organization) to get things done? How do you communicate with them—informal discussions, meetings, telephone, written reports, computer links, and so on?

*4. What kinds of problems do you have to handle at work? When problems occur, how do you handle them? (Probe for solutions that are well known versus need to discover solutions.) Do you run into many variations and unexpected situations in your work, or is it fairly similar from day to day?

5. Are there any difficulties and barriers to getting the work done here or doing it the way you would like to?

III. Group Structures and Processes—Controls, Coordinating Mechanisms (Group and Organization Levels)

1. How is the work coordinated within the unit? (Probe for the kinds of controls used, e.g., budgets, direct supervision, quality control, periodic evaluations, MBO, etc.).

2. Are goals and objectives spelled out for your unit? If so, how? (Probe for the specification of specific targets versus general direction and for the ways in which specified.)

*3. How do you know when you have done a job well? (Probe for nature of criteria, type of feedback, and time involved in feedback.)

IV. Environment—Relations to Units within the Organization (Group and Organization Levels)

1. What other units do you have to work with to get the work done? How are contacts with other units coordinated?

2. What kinds of things does your unit need to get from other units—funds, approval for action, materials, people, information, and so on? How do you get these things?

3. Are relations to other units pretty smooth and trouble-free or do uncertainties and problems arise? (If so, please describe them.)

V. Environment—External Relations (Group and Organization Levels)

1. What kinds of contacts does your unit have with external groups or organizations? (see also Question II-2) What markets or fields (areas) does your unit work/compete in? What kinds of things do people in your unit need to know about what is going on outside the organization? (Probe for important technological conditions, if not mentioned.) How do they find out?

2. What are the main kinds of resources—people, materials, services, funds, and information—you get from these groups? On which groups are you most dependent?

3. Do you run into problems and challenges in obtaining or supplying these resources and in dealing with external groups and conditions? If so, please describe them and explain how you handle them.

VI. Structure (Group and Organization Levels)

1. How is the work in this unit organized and how does the unit fit into the whole organization? (Probe for formal structure, e.g., who is the head of the unit? To whom does the head report? Who reports to the head? If appropriate, ask respondent to draw an organization chart for the unit and to show its relationship to the rest of the organization.)

2. What are the main rules or procedures in your unit that everyone has to follow? How well do they seem to work?

3. What arrangements are there for taking care of people's health, safety, and retirement needs here?

4. Are there opportunities for obtaining additional skills or training while working here?

5. Is there a union here? If so, what is the climate of union-management relations? How involved is the union in issues other than salary and benefits? (Probe for union involvement in issues such as changes in job titles, work arrangements.)

6. What other (informal) groups are there besides the official unit? (Probe for work teams, cliques, links between and within departments, groups of employees from similar ethnic backgrounds, and so on.)

VII. Processes (Group Level)

1. How do the informal groups you mentioned affect the way the work is done here? Do they get along with one another?

*2. Do you feel a part of any of these groups? If so, if you came up with a new idea or worked especially hard, how would the other people in your group(s) react?

3. Who is your supervisor—the person who is directly responsible for your work? How closely do you work with the supervisor? What is it like to work with him or her?

4. What is it like to work with the other people in you unit? (Probe for behavior indicating quality, nature of interpersonal relations, e.g., chat a lot, versus keep to themselves; help out one another.)

5. How do people find out about what is going on in the unit and in the organization as a whole? (Probe for informal and official communication channels and their use.)

6. How are decisions made in your unit? What about the organization/division as a whole—how are the decisions made that affect your unit?

*7. How much say do you have in decisions affecting your work? To what extent does your supervisor consider your opinions or consult you when making decisions affecting you? (Probe for variations by types of decisions.)

*8. Who are the really influential people in your unit? Who really controls what goes on in the organization as a whole?

9. What do you have to do to get ahead around here? Do you get rewarded for doing your job well? (Probe for kinds of rewards—pay,

promotion, praise, feeling of doing well—and the kinds of behavior which is rewarded in the unit and the organization.)

10. When people within the unit disagree about things, how are these differences resolved? (e.g., "The boss decides alone, we discuss all the sides of the question until we have the best solution, we compromise," and so on.)

VIII. Culture and Processes
(Group and Organization Levels)

*1. If you were telling a friend what it was really like to work here, how would you describe the atmosphere at work? (Probe for norms, beliefs about the nature of the work, how it should be done, and employee's involvement in work.)

2. What aspects of work are most emphasized here—quality, costs, speed, quantity, innovation, etc.?

*3. Does it pay to take risks or stick your neck out in your unit? (Probe for support for initiative, risk taking, attitudes toward criticism.)

IX. Purposes and Culture
(Group and Organizational Levels)

*1. Can you give me an example of one of your unit's major successes or achievements? What about a failure? (Probe for criteria for deciding that something succeeded or failed.)

2. What would you say is the overall mission or purpose of your organization? (or, what does your organization say it stands for?) How does the organization pursue its mission? (Probe for differences between official and actual purposes.)

3. Do you feel that your unit is operating effectively? What do you mean by effective?

X. History of Unit/Organization
(Group and Organization Levels)

1. We have talked a lot about the way things are done today in your unit. Could you tell me something about how they got this way? How have things changed since this unit got started? (Note timing of changes.)

*2. What about the organization as a whole, how has it changed?

XI. Problems and Challenges
(Group and Organization Levels)

1. What do you see as the main challenges that will be facing your unit and your organization during the next two or three years? Do you have any suggestions for how to handle them?

2. What do you feel are the main strengths of your unit? What are the strengths of the organization as a whole? What are the main problems in the unit? What are the main problems in the organization (or division) as a whole?

3. What things seem to be most in need of change in your unit? What about the organization as a whole? (Probe for reasons for mentioning these problems.)

XII. Individual Satisfactions

*1. (If not already evident—)In general how satisfied are you with working here? What things make you feel most satisfied? What are the things with which you are least satisfied?

APPENDIX B

Three Major Instruments

These instruments are long, research-based questionnaires with many subscales. Technical information (e.g., scale construction, reliability, validity) and advice on administration are contained in the published sources. Practitioners may select among these scales or choose items from within scales. Permission to reproduce or use these and other instruments should be obtained from their publishers.

Michigan Organizational Assessment Questionnaire (MOAQ). MOAQ (Cammann et al., 1983) covers a wide range of individual-level attitudes and beliefs that can be averaged to obtain group-level data (see Chapter 3). See Seashore et al. (1983) for information on other instruments in the Michigan Quality of Work Life Program. Readers may contact Dr. Cortland Cammann for more recent information on these instruments (Institute for Social Research, Ann Arbor, MI 48104).

Organizational Assessment Inventory (OAI). OAI (Van de Ven & Ferry, 1980) is a family of questionnaires that provide sophisticated, sometimes complex, measures of processes, structures, technologies, and relations to external units (see Chapter 3 and Van de Ven & Ferry, 1980, for overviews). For information on recent revisions research using OAI contact Professor Andrew Van de Ven, School of Management, University of Minnesota, Minneapolis, 55455.

Survey of Organizations. This machine-scored instrument measures the following sets of variables that Likert (1967) and his associates identified as the strongest predictors of employee satisfaction and performance:

—Organizational Climate (respondents' perceptions of organizational processes such as communication flows, decision-making processes, conflict resolution; the extent to which work facilitated, and the basis for motivation to work)

1. Information on the status of these instrument as of early 1985 was graciously provided by Professors Stanley Seashore (MOAQ), Andrew Van de Ven (OAI), J. Richard Hackman (JDS), and by Mr. David Summers (Goodmeasure).

—Supervisory Behavior (support, work facilitation, interaction facilitation, and goal emphasis)
—Peer Relationships (variables are parallel to those for supervisors)
—Group Processes (trust, communication, decision making, flexibility, etc.)

In addition, there are a range of measures of satisfaction. See Taylor and Bowers (1972) for extensive methodological documentation and Hausser et al. (1975) on using the survey in organization development projects. The major drawbacks of the instrument are its reliance on a model of organizational effectiveness that is no longer regarded as universally valid and its exclusive use of subjective, attitudinal questions, which are especially prone to response biases (see Chapter 3).
The instrument has not been revised or updated since 1972. For additional information contact Rensis Likert Associates, 3001 S. State St., Ann Arbor, MI 48104.

Brief Instruments

Here are examples of short questionnaires that can be helpful in signaling problem areas or for gathering data for self-diagnosis and problem solving:
Group Effectiveness Survey. This 25-item questionnaire (Nadler, 1977, pp. 194–198) elicits generalizations about such internal organizational features as group tasks, processes (conflict, leadership, interpersonal relations, etc.)—for example, "How much conflict is expressed in your group?" Questions also cover satisfaction and five aspects of group effectiveness. A computerized feedback form is shown, but no technical information is provided.
Organizational Diagnosis Questionnaire. Perziosi (1980) provides 35 items on respondents' evaluations of their organization with regard to 6 areas: purposes, structure, relationships, leadership, rewards, and coordinating mechanisms (see Weisbord, 1978). No technical data are provided.
Job Diagnostic Survey (JDS) and the Job Rating Form (JRF). JDS (Hackman and Oldham, 1980) focuses specifically on job characteristics that affect motivation (see Chapter 3). Questions cover:

—Job Characteristics (skill variety, task identity, task significance, feedback, autonomy)

—Psychological States (meaningfulness of work, sense of responsibility, and knowledge of the actual results; satisfaction with job and work context, and respondents' need for growth at work)

JRF is a companion measure in which supervisors describe their subordinates' jobs. These instruments, which were used extensively in research, appear in Hackman and Oldham (1980), along with instructions for their administration, national norms for each variable, and discussions of their theoretical basis and their use in programs of job redesign. A short form of JDS is also available. The authors of JDS are no longer working on the instrument.

Other instruments. Shorter instruments are often reported in academic journals (see Appendix C) and are sometimes available from consulting firms. For example, Goodmeasure Inc. (Directors: Dr. R. Kanter and B. Stein, 330 Broadway PO Box 3004 Cambridge, MA 02139) developed Power Dimensions in Your Job, an instrument that could be used in training or action planning or adapted for use in diagnosing power relations. The firm also makes available parts of Assessment of Organizational Character, an instrument for assessing features associated with innovation (Kanter, 1983).

Many other focused diagnostic instruments have been published in the *Annual: Developing Human Resources* (previously titled *Annual Handbook for Group Facilitators and Consultants)*. However, the articles prior to 1984 do not provide any theoretical background for the instruments, and in no case are technical data on reliability and validity given. Most of these instruments are brief questionnaires designed to be used in workshops or training sessions where participants engage in self-diagnosis with the help of a consultant or trainer. Many are designed to provide diagnostic data for use in team building. For example, Costigan and Schmeidler (1984) give measures for diagnosing the climate of group communication and conflict resolution (e.g., extent to which the atmosphere is judgmental and authoritarian, supportive of worker participation, and encourages free and open exchange of information and constructive conflict resolution). Another useful instrument in the *Annual* is a questionnaire for measuring the feelings and conditions concerning the quality of work life (Sashkin & Lengerman, 1984.)

APPENDIX C

WHERE TO GET TRAINING AND EXPERIENCE IN ORGANIZATIONAL DIAGNOSIS

Academic training. Social and behavioral science departments and professional schools offer many courses relating to organizations and organizational behavior that can equip students with methods and conceptual frames that are useful in diagnosis and a smaller number of courses on applied research and organization development. Concentrations in organizational behavior are often available in schools of management. Courses in statistics and quantitative research techniques are widely offered, whereas, nonquantitative research techniques, such as unstructured observation and open interviewing, are most often taught in departments of anthropology and sociology.

Workshops, seminars, and conferences. Many universities offer evening courses that are often more practically oriented than courses for credit. Workshops, seminars, and conferences are also sponsored by many of the professional and academic organizations which have sections devoted to organizational studies or applied organizational work—for example, the American Psychological Association.

Three organizations offer a wide variety of courses and workshops throughout the United States and Canada in organization development, including training in diagnosis. They provide opportunities for experiential learning of skills like giving and receiving feedback and team building:

—The National Training Laboratories (PO Box 9155 Rosslyn Sta., Arlington VA 22209) is the largest and oldest of the organizations that applied the approach of sensitivity training to organization development. NTL programs have become very diverse but still retain an emphasis on sensitivity training and experiential learning.
—University Associates Publishers and Consultants (8517 Production Ave. PO Box 26240, San Diego CA 92126) offers a broad range of workshops and training programs, publishes many materials on organization development, and holds annual conferences.
—The Organization Development Institute (11234 Walnut Ridge Rd., Chesterland OH 44026) sponsors a variety of local, national, and international conferences and publishes an *International Registry of Organization Development Professionals.*

This listing is not intended to imply approval or recommendation of any particular course or program.

Readers may also wish to inquire whether local applied behavioral science consulting firms offer any workshops or training programs in organization development and diagnosis. Names of local firms may be obtained from university professors specializing in organizational research; the listings under Management Consultants in the Yellow Pages; the list of firms in the *1983 Annual for Facilitators, Trainers, and Consultants;* and the Organization Development Institute's registry of professionals.

For further reading. Those who want to read further on their own in fields like organizational behavior, diagnosis, and organization development can begin with basic texts (e.g., Gordon, 1983; Huse & Cummings, 1985; Miles, 1980) and then consult the references to this book. Journals for keeping abreast of academic developments include:

—*Annual Review of Sociology*
—*Annual Review of Psychology*
—*Review of Organizational Behavior*
—*Administrative Science Quarterly*
—*Academy of Management Review*

Periodicals with a more applied emphasis include:

—*Organizational Dynamics*
—*Journal of Applied Behavioral Sciences*
—*Annual: Developing Human Resources*
—*Harvard Business Review*
—*Sloan Management Review*
—Business periodicals (e.g.,*Business Week, Fortune)*

REFERENCES

Abrahamsson, B. (1977). *Bureaucracy or participation: The logic of organization.* Beverly Hills, CA: Sage.

Alderfer, C. (1977). Organization development. *Annual Review of Psychology, 28,* 197–223.

Alinsky, S. (1971). *Rules for radicals.* New York: Random House/Vintage Books.

Andrews, K. (1971). *The concept of corporate strategy.* Homewood, IL: Dow-Jones, Irwin.

Argyris, C. (1970). *Intervention theory and method.* Reading, MA: Addison-Wesley.

Argyris, C. and Schon, D. (1978). *Organizational learning: A theory of action perspective:* Reading, MA: Addison-Wesley.

Austin, M. (1982). *Evaluating your agency's programs.* Beverly Hills, CA: Sage.

Beckhard, R. (1969). *Organization development: Strategies and models:* Reading, MA: Addison-Wesley.

Beckhard, R., and Harris, R. (1975). Strategies for large system change. *Sloan Management Review, 16,* 43–55.

Beckhard, R. and Harris, R. (1977). *Organizational transitions: Managing complex change.* Reading, MA: Addison-Wesley.

Beer, M. (1980). *Organizational change and development—A systems view.* Santa Monica, CA: Goodyear.

Benne, K. and Sheats, P. (1948). Functional roles of group members. *Journal of Social Issues, 2,* 42–47

Bennis, W. et al. (1976). *The planning of change.* (3rd ed.). New York: Holt, Rinehart and Winston.

Blake, R. and Mouton, J. (1964). *The managerial grid.* Houston: Gulf.

Blau, P. (1955). *Dynamics of bureaucracy.* Chicago, IL: University of Chicago Press.

Block, P. (1982). *Flawless consulting.* San Diego. CA: University Associates.

Bowditch, J., and Buono, A. (1982). *Quality of work life assessment.* Boston, MA: Auburn.

Bowen, D. (1977). Value dilemmas in organization development. *Journal of Applied Behavioral Science, 13,* 543–556.

Burke, W. W. (1982). *Organization development.* Boston, MA: Little, Brown.

Burns, T. (1961). Micropolitics: Mechanisms of institutional change. *Administrative Science Quarterly, 6,* 257–281.

Burns, T., and Stalker, G. M. (1961). *The management of innovation.* London: Tavistock.

Business Week. (1981a). The new industrial relations. May 11, 1981, 85–93.

Business Week. (1981b). The new Sears: Unable to grow in retailing, it turns to financial services. (International Edition) November 16, 110–114.

Cameron, K. (1980). Critical questions in assessing organizational effectiveness. *Organization Dynamics, 9,* 66–80.

Cammann, C. et al. (1983). Assessing the attitudes and perceptions of members. In S. Seashore et al. (Eds.), *Assessing organizational change* (pp. 71–138). New York: John Wiley.

Campbell, D. (1977). On the nature of organizational effectiveness. In P. Goodman and J. Pennings (Eds.), *New perspectives on organizational effectiveness* (pp. 13–55). San Francisco, CA: Jossey-Bass.

Cannell, C., and Kahn, R. (1968). Interviewing. In G. Lindzey and E. Aronson (Eds.), *Handbook of social psychology.* (2nd ed. pp. 526–595). Reading, MA: Addison-Wesley.

Carlisle, H. (1974). A contingency approach to decentralization. *Advanced Management Journal,* July.

Chesler, M., Crawfoot, J., and Bryant, B. (1978). Power training: An alternative path to conflict management. *California Management Review, 21,* 84–91.

Child, J. (1972). Organization structure, environment, and performance: The role of strategic choice. *Sociology, 6,* 1–22.

Child, J. (1977). *Organization: A guide to problems and practice.* New York: Harper and Row.

Costigan, J., and Schmeidler, M. (1984). Exploring supportive and defensive communication climates. In J. Pfeiffer and L. Goodstein (Eds.), *The 1984 annual: Developing human resources* (pp. 112–118), San Diego, CA: University Associates.

Davis, L., and Cherns, A. (1975). *The quality of working life.* (Vols. 1 and 2). New York: Free Press.

Davis, S. (1984). *Managing corporate culture.* Cambridge, MA: Ballinger.

Davis, S., and Lawrence, P. in collaboration with Kolondny and Beer. (1977). *Matrix.* Reading, MA: Addison-Wesley.

Fishbein, M., and Ajzen, I. (1975). *Beliefs, attitudes, intention, and behavior.* Reading, MA: Addison-Wesley.

Fottler, M. (1981). Is management really generic? *Academy of Management Review, 6,* 1–12.

Fry, R. (1982). Improving trustee, administrator, and physician collaboration through open systems planning. In M. Plovnick et al. (Eds.), *Organization development: Exercises, cases and readings* (pp. 282–292), Boston, MA: Little Brown.

Galbraith, J. (1977). *Organization design.* Reading, MA: Addison-Wesley.

Goffman, E. (1959). *The presentation of self in everyday life.* Garden City, NY: Doubleday.

Goodman, P. S. (1977). Social comparison processes. In B. Staw and G. Salancik (Eds.), *New directions in organizational behavior.* Chicago: St. Clair.

Goodman, P. S., and Pennings, J. (1980). Critical issues in assessing organizational effectiveness. In E. Lawler et al. (Eds.), *Organizational assessment* (pp. 185–215), New York: Wiley.

Gordon, J. (1983). *A diagnostic approach to organizational behavior.* Boston: Allyn and Bacon.

Hackman, R., and Oldham, G. (1980). *Work redesign.* Reading, MA: Addison-Wesley.

Hall, R. (1982). *Organizations, structure and process* (2nd ed.). Englewood Cliffs, NG: Prentice-Hall.

Harrison, R. (1970). Choosing the depth of organizational intervention. *Journal of Applied Behavioral Science, 6,* 181–202.

Hausser, C., Pecorella, P., and Wissler, A. (1975). *Survey guided development: A manual for consultants.* Ann Arbor: Institute for Social Research, University of Michigan.

Hayes, R., and Abernathy, W. (1980). Managing our way to economic decline. *Harvard Business Review, 58,* 67–77.

Hedberg, B. (1981). How organizations learn and unlearn. In P. Nystrom and W. Starbuck (Eds.), *Handbook of organizational design* (Vol. 1, pp. 1–27). New York: Oxford University Press.

Huff, A. (1980). Organizations as political systems: Implications for diagnosis, change and stability. In T. G. Cummings (Eds.), *Systems theory for organization development* (pp. 163-180). Chichester, England: John Wiley.

Huse, E., and Cummings. T. (1985). *Organization development* (3rd ed.). St. Paul, MN: West.

Izraeli, D.N. (1975). The middle manager and tactics of power expansion—A case study. *Sloan Management Review*, 16, 57-70.

Jayaram, G. K. (1976). Open systems planning. In W. G. Bennis, et al. (Eds.), *The planning of change*, (3rd ed. pp. 275-28). New York,: Holt, Rinehart and Winston.

Kanter, R. (1977). *Men and women of the corporation.* New York: Basic.

Kanter, R. (1979). Power failure in management circuits. *Harvard Business Review, 57,* 65-75.

Kanter, R. (1983). *The change masters: Innovation for productivity in the American corporation.* New York: Simon and Schuster.

Kanter, R., and Brinkerhoff, D. (1981). Organizational performance. *Annual Review of Sociology, 7,* 321-349.

Katz, D., and Kahn, R. (1978). *The social psychology of organizations* (2nd ed.). New York: John Wiley.

Katz, D., and Kahn, R. (1980). Organization as social systems. In E. Lawler et al. (Eds.), *Organizational assessment.* (pp. 162-184). New York: John Wiley.

Kets de Vries, M. (1979). Organizational stress: A call for management action. *Sloan Management Review, 21,* 3-14.

Khandwalla, P. (1977). *The design of organizations.* New York: Harcourt Brace Jovanovich.

Kidder, T. (1981). *The soul of a new machine.* Boston: Little, Brown.

Kolb, D., and Frohman, A. (1970). An organization development approach to consulting. *Sloan Management Review, 12,* 51-65.

Kotter, J. (1978). *Organizational dynamics.* Reading, MA: Addison-Wesley.

Lauffer, R. et al. (1977). *Understanding your social agency.* Beverly Hills, CA: Sage.

Lauffer, R. et al. (1982). *Assessment tools: For practitioners, managers, trainers.* Beverly Hills, CA: Sage.

Lawler, E. (1977). Reward systems. In J. Hackman & J. Suttle (Eds.), *Improving life at work: Behavioral science approaches to organizational change* (pp. 166-226). Santa Monica, CA: Goodyear.

Lawler, E. and Drexler, J. (1980). Participative research: The subject as co-researcher. In E. Lawler et al. (Eds.), *Organization assessment* (pp. 535-547). New York: John Wiley.

Lawler, E., Nadler, D., and Cammann, C. (Eds.). (1980). *Organizational assessment.* New York: John Wiley.

Lawler, E., Nadler, D., and Mirvis, P. (1983). Organizational change and the conduct of organizational research. In E. Lawler et al. (Eds.), *Assessing organizational change* (pp. 19-48). New York: John Wiley.

Lawler, E., and Rhode, J. (1976). *Information and control in organizations.* Santa Monica, CA: Goodyear.

Lawrence, P., and Lorsch, J. (1969). *Organization and environment* Homewood, IL: Irwin.

Leach, J. (1979). The organizational history: A consulting analysis and intervention tool. In G. Gore and R. Wright (Eds.), *The academic consultant connection* (pp. 62-69). Dubuque, IA: Kendall/Hunt.

Levinson, H. (1972). *Organizational diagnosis.* Cambridge, MA: Harvard University Press.

Likert. R. (1967). *The human organization.* New York: McGraw-Hill.

Lofland, J. (1971). *Analyzing social situations.* Belmont, CA: Wadsworth.

Lorsch, J., and Morse, J. (1974). *Organizations and their members: A contingency approach.* New York: Harper and Row.

McCaskey, M. (1979). A contingency approach to planning. *Academy of Management Journal, 17,* 281-291.

McGregor, D. (1960). *The human side of enterprise.* New York: McGraw-Hill.

Meyer, J., and Rowan, B. (1977). Institutionalized organizations: Formal structure as myth and ceremony. *American Journal of Sociology,* 83, *340-363.*

Miles, R. E., and Snow, C. (1978). *Organizational strategy, structure, and process.* New York: McGraw-Hill.

Miles. R. H. (1980). *Macro organizational behavior.* Santa Monica, CA: Goodyear.

Mintzberg, H. (1979). *The structuring of organizations.* Englewood Cliffs, NJ: Prentice-Hall.

Mintzberg, H. (1983). *Power in and around organizations.* Englewood Cliffs, NJ: Prentice-Hall.

Mirvis, P., and Seashore, S. (1980). Being ethical on organizational research. In E. Lawler et al. (Eds.), *Organizational assessment* (pp. 583-612). New York: John Wiley.

Moch, M., Cammann, C., and Cooke, R. (1983a). Organizational structure: Measuring the degree of influence. In S. Seashore et al. (Eds.), *Assessing organizational change* (pp. 177-202). New York: John Wiley.

Moch, M., Feather, J., and Fitzgibbons , D. (1983b). Conceptualizing and measuring the relational structure of organizations. In S. Seashore et al. (Eds.), *Assessing organizational change* (pp. 203-228). New York: John Wiley.

Nadler, D. (1977). *Feedback and organization development: Using data-based methods.* Reading, MA: Addison-Wesley.

Nadler, D., Mirvis, P., and Cammann, C. (1976). The ongoing feedback system: Experimenting with a new management tool. *Organizational Dynamics. 4,* 63-80.

Nadler, D., and Tushman, M. (1980a). A congruence model for diagnosing organizational behavior. In E. Lawler et al. (Eds.), *Organizational assessment* (pp. 261-278). New York: John Wiley.

Nadler, D., and Tushman, M. (1980b). A model for diagnosing organizational behavior. *Organizational Dynamics, 9,* 35-51.

Newman, W., and Warren, E. (1977). *The process of management.* Englewood Cliffs, NJ: Prentice-Hall.

Nightingale, O., and Toulouse, J. (1977). Toward a multi-level congruence theory of organization. *Administrative Science Quarterly, 22,* 264-280.

O'Conner, P. (1977). A critical inquiry into some assumptions and values characterizing O.D. *Academy of Management* Review. 2, 635-644.

Ouchi, W. (1981). *Theory Z.* Reading, MA: Addison-Wesley.

Pasmore, W., and Sherwood, J. (Eds.). (1978). *Socio-technical systems: A source book.* San Diego, CA: University Associates.

Pennings, J., and Goodman, P. (1977). Toward a workable framework. In P. Goodman and J. Pennings (Eds.), *New perspectives on organizational effectiveness* (pp. 164-184). San Francisco, CA: Jossey-Bass.

Perkins, D., Nadler, D., and Hanlon, M. (1981). A method for structured naturalistic observation of organizational behavior. In J. Pfeiffer and J. Jones (Eds.), *The 1981 annual handbook for group facilitators* (pp. 222-244). San Diego, CA: University Associates.

Perrow, C. (1970). *Organizational analysis: A sociological view.* Belmont, CA: Wadsworth.

Perziosi, R. (1980). Organizational diagnosis questionnaire (ODQ). In J. Pfeiffer and J. Jones (Eds.), *The 1981 annual handbook for group facilitators.* (pp. 112-120). San Diego, CA: University Associates.

Pfeffer, J. (1981a). Management as symbolic action: The creation and management of organizational paradigms. *Research in Organizational Behavior, 3,* 1-52.

Pfeffer, J. (1981b). *Power in organizations.* Marshfield, MA: Pitman.

Pfeffer, J.,and Salancik, G. (1978). *The external control of organizations.* New York: Harper & Row.

Plovnick, M., Fry, R., & Burke, W. (1982). *Organization development: Exercises, cases and readings.* Boston, MA: Little, Brown.

Pondy, L. (1967). Organizational conflict: Concepts and models *Administrative Science Quarterly, 12,* 296-320.

Porras, J., and Berg, P. (1978). The impact of organizational development. *Academy of Management Review, 3,* 249-266.

Porter, L., Allen R., and Angle, H. (1981). The politics of upward influence in organizations. *Research in Organizational Behavior, 3,* 109-150.

Porter, M. (1980). *Competitive strategy: Techniques for analyzing industries and competitors.* New York: Free Press.

President and Fellows of Harvard College. (1980). *Action planning and implementation: A manager's checklist.* No. 9-481-010. Boston: HBS Case Services.

Price, J. (1972). *Handbook of organizational measurement.* Lexington, MA: D. C. Heath.

Quinn, J. B. (1977). Strategic goals: Process and politics. *Sloan Management Review, 19,* 21-37.

Quinn, J.B. (1980). *Strategies for change: Logical incrementalism.* Homewood, IL: Irwin.

Robbins, S. P. (1978). Conflict management and conflict resolution are not synonymous terms. *California Management Review, 21,* 67-75.

Rossi, P., and Freeman, H. (1982). *Evaluation: A systematic approach* (2nd ed.). Beverly Hills, CA: Sage.

Salancik, G., and Pfeffer, J. (1977). An examination of need satisfaction models of job attitudes. *Administrative Science Quarterly, 22,* 427-456.

Sashkin, M., and Lengerman, J. (1984). Quality of work life-conditions/feelings. In J. Pfeiffer and L. Goodstein (Eds.), *The 1984 annual: Developing human resources* (pp. 131-144). San Diego, CA: University Associates.

Sayles, L. (1979). *Leadership.* New York: McGraw-Hill.

Schatzman, L., and Strauss, A. (1973). *Field methods.* Englewood Cliffs, NJ: Prentice-Hall.

Schein, E. (1969). *Process consultation: its role in organization development.* Reading, MA: Addison-Wesley.

Schon, D. (1983). *The reflective practitioner—How professionals think in action.* New York: Basic Books.

Seashore, S., Lawler, E., Mirvis, P., and Cammann, C. (Eds.). (1983). *Assessing organizational change.* New York: John Wiley.

Sellitiz, C. et al. (1981). *Research methods in social relations* (3rd ed.). New York: Holt, Rinehart and Winston.

Steele, F. (1973). *Physical settings and organization development.* Reading, MA: Addison-Wesley.

Steele, F. (1975). *Consulting for organization change.* Amherst, MA: University of Massachusetts Press.

Strauss, G. (1976). Organizational development. In R. Dubin (Ed.), *Handbook of work, organization, and society* (pp. 617–363). Santa Monica, CA: Goodyear.

Strauss, G.(1977). Managerial practices. In J. Hackman and T. Suttle (Eds.), *Improving life at work.* (pp. 297–363). Santa Monica, CA:Goodyear

Strauss, G. (1982). Worker's participation in management: An international perspective. *Research in Organizational Behavior. 4,* 173–265.

Sutherland, J. (Ed). (1978). *Management handbook for public administrators.* New York: Van Nostrand.

Tannenbuam, A. S. (1968). *Control in organizations.* New York: McGraw-Hill.

Taylor, J., and Bowers, D. (1972). *Survey of organizations: A machine scored standardized questionnaire instrument.* Ann Arbor, MI: Institute for Social Research, University of Michigan.

Thompson, J. (1967). *Organizations in action.* New York: McGraw-Hill.

Tichy, N. (1978). Diagnosis for complex health care delivery systems: A model and case study. *Journal of Applied Behavioral Science, 14,* 305–320.

Tichy, N. (1983). *Managing strategic change: Technical, political and cultural dynamics.* New York: John Wiley.

Tichy, N., Tushman, M., and Fombrun (1980). Network analysis in organizations. In E. Lawler et al. (Eds.), *Organizational assessment* (pp. 372–398). New York: John Wiley.

Tilles, S. (1961). Understanding the consultant's role. *Harvard Business Review, 39,* 87–99.

Torbert, W. (1981). The role of self-study in improving managerial and institutional effectiveness. *Human Systems Management, 2,* 72–82.

Turner, A. (1982). Consulting is more than giving advice. *Harvard Business Review, 60,* 120–129.

Tushman, M. (1977). A political approach to organization: A review and rationale. *Academy of Management Review, 3,* 613–624.

Tushman, M., and Nadler, D. (1978). Information processing as an integrative concept in organizational design. *Academy of Management Review, 2,* 206–216.

Van de Ven, A., and Drazen, R. (1985). The concept of fit in contingency theory. *Research in Organizational Behavior, 7,* 333-365.

Van de Ven, A., and Ferry, D. (1980). *Measuring and assessing organizations.* New York: John Wiley.

Walton, R. (1975). Quality of working life: What is it? *Sloan Management Review, 15,* 11–21.

Walton, R., and Dutton, J. (1969). The management of interdepartmental conflict: A model and review. *Administrative Science Quarterly, 14,* 73–84.

Walton, R., and Warwick, D. (1973). The ethics of organization development. *Journal of Applied Behavioral Science, 9,* 681–698.

Webb. E. et al. (1966). *Unobtrusive measures: Non-reactive research in the social sciences.* Chicago, IL: Rand McNally.

Weick, K. (1979). *The social psychology of organizing* (2nd ed.) Reading, MA: Addison-Wesley.

Weick, K. (1985). Systematic observation methods. In G. Lindzey and E. Aronson (eds.). *Hardbook of Social Psychology* (3rd ed.). Vol. 2 (pp. 567-634), Reading MA: Addison-Wesley.

Weisbord, M. (1978). *Organizational diagnosis: A workbook of theory and practice.* Reading, MA: Addison-Wesley.

Wildavsky, A. (1972). The self-evaluating organization. *Public Administration Review, 32,* 509-520.

Zald, M., and Berger, M. (1978). Social movements in organizations: Coup d'etat, insurgency, and mass novements. *American Journal of Sociology, 83,* 823-861.

INDEX

INDEX 159

teams 6, 71
Workers 7, 93, 101
Working conditions 34, 52, 54
Workshops 1, 3, 6, 18, 21, 76, 98, 113, 119

Youth agency 9
Youth Services Division 103

ABOUT THE AUTHOR

Michael I. Harrison is a Senior Lecturer at Bar Ilan University in Ramat Gan, Israel, where he has been a faculty member since 1974. He served as Chairperson of the Department of Sociology and Anthropology there and currently heads its graduate Program in Organizational Sociology. Since 1981 he has been an Adjunct Associate Professor in the Department of Organization Studies/Human Resources Management of the School of Management, Boston College, where he has also served as a Visiting Associate Professor. During 1980–1981 he was a Visiting Scholar at the Graduate School of Business of Harvard University. He is active in the Israeli and American Sociological Associations and the Academy of Management. Originally from New York, Professor Harrison received his B.A. in sociology from Columbia College in 1966 and his Ph.D. in sociology in 1972 from the University of Michigan, where he was a National Science Foundation Fellow. From 1970 to 1974 he was a member of the Sociology Department at SUNY, Stony Brook. Professor Harrison has worked as a consultant and conducted research in businesses, service and governmental organizations, worker-managed cooperatives, and voluntary groups working for social and political change. His research on organizations, social conflicts and movements, and on social institutions in America and Israel has been published in leading academic journals and has been presented at numerous academic meetings. His current research deals with managerial planning and problem solving, mobilization processes in social conflicts, and professional unionism.